# JESUS WAS A MIGRANT

# JESUS WAS A MIGRANT

**Deirdre Cornell**

ORBIS BOOKS

**Maryknoll, New York 10545**

ORBIS BOOKS
Maryknoll, New York 10545

Fathers and Brothers
MARYKNOLL™

Founded in 1970, Orbis Books endeavors to publish works that enlighten the mind, nourish the spirit, and challenge the conscience. The publishing arm of the Maryknoll Fathers & Brothers, Orbis seeks to explore the global dimensions of the Christian faith and mission, to invite dialogue with diverse cultures and religious traditions, and to serve the cause of reconciliation and peace. The books published reflect the views of their authors and do not represent the official position of the Maryknoll Society. To learn more about Maryknoll and Orbis Books, please visit our website at www.maryknollsociety.org.

Manufactured in the United States of America.
Manuscript editing and typesetting by Joan Weber Laflamme.

**Library of Congress Cataloging-in-Publication Data**

Cornell, Deirdre.
    Jesus was a migrant / Deirdre Cornell.
      pages cm
    Includes bibliographical references.
    ISBN 978-1-62698-040-2
    1. Emigration and immigration—Religious aspects—Christianity.
2. Emigration and immigration—Religious aspects—Catholic Church.
3. Church work with immigrants—United States. 4. Church work with immigrants—Catholic Church. I. Title.
BV639.I4C67 2014
261.8'36—dc23

2013037322

*Daniel Dennis Crimmins,*
*son of Irish immigrants,*
*Christian Brother and Abuelito*

# Contents

## PART III

## PART IV

# In Appreciation

I like to think this book about spirituality and migration describes a journey of faith.

My parents, brother, and husband have given me the witness of their lives, shaped by the Catholic Worker movement, which "welcomes the stranger." I value their example more with each passing year. My wonderful in-laws, with their warm hospitality, give generously of "the pearl of great price." My husband and children—with whom I am at home, wherever we are—never let me forget that "where you treasure is, there your heart will be also."

This book contains reflections on sacred scripture and my experience working with migrants and immigrants. Over two decades my husband and I were privileged to share deeply in the lives of people who opened our eyes to the challenges they faced in seeking a better future. These reflections were written over a period of twelve years; portions of earlier versions were printed in *The Catholic Worker.* Biblical quotations follow the New Revised Standard Version. Translations from Spanish are mine. In order to present realities while not exposing individuals' lives, I changed names and details and created composite characters.

I am very grateful to the pastors and religious who allowed me to contribute to their ministry, and to the many organizations that advocate for immigrants. My husband and I were especially honored to serve in a pastoral project for farm workers led by Brother Dan Crimmins, CFC; Fr. Tomás Bobadilla and Sr. Martha Hernández, OLC, gave so much to this labor, as does Fr. Tom (Martín) Deely, CSsR, a Redemptorist with fifty years of mission experience. I am most indebted to the newcomers from diverse countries of origin who enliven our common Christian faith. They have been my greatest teachers.

In writing, my thinking was stimulated by a National Workshop on Human Mobility in Mexico; an Immigration Summit at Mariandale, New York; the Rita McGinley Symposium at Duquesne University; the 2010 Religious Education Congress in Anaheim, California; the Grail International Conference in the Netherlands and its Theological Resources meeting in Portugal; the Commission on the Status of Women at the United Nations in New York; the exhibition "Race: Are We So Different?" hosted by the Smithsonian Institution in Washington DC; events of the Mexican Studies Institute at the City University of New York; and a conference of Mano a Mano and the Archdiocese of New York at Fordham University. At these gatherings, I benefitted from hearing from people whose tremendous work inspires great hope. Closer to home, I would like to thank members of Hermanos Unidos, Brazos Abiertos, Misión Guadalupana, and the Grail Centers at Cornwall and the South Bronx.

Conversations with and presentations by Juan Carlos Aguirre, Sr. María Teresa de Bourbon, RDC, Dr. Ilze Earner, Robert Fuchs, Esq., Dr. Alyshia Galvez, Fr. Daniel Groody, CSC, Mario Russell, Esq., Juan Carlos Ruíz, Dr. Robert Smith, Fr. Alejandro Solalinde, and Diana Vázquez contributed in various ways to my understanding of human mobility. Fr. Tom Welbers and Dr. John Downey graciously sent research suggestions. Fr. Eugene LaVerdiere, SSS, influenced my study of scripture. Dr. Eva Fleischner shared her insight into the psalms. Maryknoll missioners, Grail members, and Catholic Workers are ongoing sources of inspiration. Grupo Folklorico of Poughkeepsie, New York, allowed me to use its photographs.

Finally, I wish to thank Mike Leach at Orbis Books, who invited me to write another book—and who, for the third time, christened it with a title!

# PART I

*And Jesus said . . . "Foxes have holes, and birds of the air have nests; but the Son of Man has nowhere to lay his head."*

—MATTHEW 8:20

The Flight into Egypt (by an anonymous Coptic artist)

# Chapter One

# Migrants Matter

I have been blessed through migrants and immigrants.

It started off simply. As college graduates my husband and I went to Mexico to volunteer for a year (which is how we met). Over subsequent visits we stayed in poor neighborhoods and villages with friends who opened their hearts and homes to us and then, to our young children. We were deeply moved by the truism that people who owned so little gave so much. Returning to the United States, we wanted to reciprocate that generosity. We hoped to make a small return of the hospitality we received abundantly in Mexico.

In the state of New York we volunteered for a faith-based project for agricultural workers, many of whom travel with the seasons. For a time we lived in an inner city. Accompanying immigrant families, in both rural and urban settings, acquainted us with the difficulties in their lives. We also experimented with offering hospitality to recently arrived immigrants in our home. My husband took an outreach position in social services, serving the needs of the farm-worker population. He has held that job for many years with commitment.

Taking a brief respite, we served as lay missioners in Mexico (where our two youngest children were born). There my husband helped start a health-promoters program for a medical clinic. After three years we returned with our children to the United States.

My background in theology and religious education was put to use in ministry. I was impressed with the priests, religious, and lay leaders who sought out recently arrived immigrants—and with the newcomers themselves who joined enthusiastically in mission outreach. I assisted in sacramental preparation, a radio show, youth groups, bereavement work, immigration advocacy, and catechism. Pastoral efforts allowed me to set my footsteps alongside theirs on a shared path: our journey of faith. As I reflected on the liturgy and the word through the lens of these experiences, I came to know Christ more deeply.

My husband and I consider ourselves extremely fortunate to be godparents to many children. In this role I have entered into even more intimate conversations with immigrant parents. We have *compadres* (parents of our godchildren) who pick corn or apples and travel with the crops. We also have *compadres* who are high-earning professionals, well educated in their chosen fields, with the ability to move internationally as they please. I have benefitted from these relationships immensely and remain forever grateful.

Beyond those pertaining to my own family, the most poignant moments I have experienced were spent with immigrants who welcomed us into their lives even as we welcomed them to our country. On occasion we got to rejoice with illiterate parents as they saw their children graduate (the first in their families to access higher education). We watched newcomers achieve residency, then citizenship, proudly becoming new Americans: full members of society.

On a more somber note we witnessed sufferings and setbacks. We shared the distress of families when their loved ones were detained. We became part of a circle of groups responding to desperate needs. And, like anyone who has loved, I was changed. I have wept at tragedies that broke my heart—broke it wide open.

Although the configuration of my family background was determined by my ancestors' decision to leave Europe, while I was growing up I never thought much about the fact that my forebears were themselves immigrants. But when my husband and I felt called to serve migrants and immigrants, our own small corner of the planet was enlarged. My view of human mobility began to change. Furthermore, my understanding of its role in salvation history was utterly transformed. Migration has been, for centuries, not only a source of controversy but a source of blessing.

✢ ✢ ✢

The Judeo-Christian tradition holds a rich treasury of memories in which the journey of God's Chosen People is shaped by individual and collective migrations. The incarnation and the paschal mystery—for believers, the most radical and decisive moments of human history—can be understood more deeply in continuity with this aspect of biblical spirituality.

Jesus belonged to a people indelibly marked by stories of Exodus and exile. His life and ministry are framed by these narratives. When Jesus' first followers called themselves people of the Way, they were following the trajectory of Jewish scriptural spirituality. For two millennium, as Christians have interiorized the great biblical stories of human mobility, migration has figured prominently in our faith.

During the troubled past century, faith-based organizations pioneered efforts for humane resettlement of refugees and advocated for migrants and immigrants. They continue to play these roles, compelled by religious conviction. The beautiful tradition of "repairing the world" (*tikkun olam* in Hebrew) comes alive. One church has spoken of this labor—like all ministry—as God's work carried out by our hands.[1] Religious leaders of many Christian denominations address the contemporary challenge of immigration. They differ in their stances toward specific policies. Yet, most statements (along with those of interfaith counterparts) reveal a consensus of compassion.

In various countries and communities immigration has become a thorny and divisive issue. More than ever before in human history families leave their places of origin in search of a better life. According to the International Organization for Migration

---

[1] This lovely expression belongs to the Evangelical Lutheran Church in America.

(established in 1951 to help resettle refugees from World War II), today over two hundred million people are migrants or immigrants. This is equivalent to the population of Brazil, the world's fifth largest nation. Displacement in some parts of the planet has reached crisis levels, posing concerns for people of all faith backgrounds. The World Council of Churches—which comprises hundreds of denominations in 110 countries—lists migration as a priority for its programs.

Religious adherents plumb our traditions for ways to "move ahead" in our globalized societies. Catholic Christians inherit a legacy of social teaching elaborated in bishops' letters and papal encyclicals, initiated in modern times by *Rerum novarum* in 1891 and continuing into the present. These documents enlarge our parochial scope to a global panorama.

Through the documents of the Second Vatican Council, the Catholic Church reiterated one expression of its self-understanding, namely, as the people of God on pilgrimage. This wording uses pilgrimage—an intentional journey—to describe the very heart of what it means to be believers. The mystery of the Father's revelation of Christ to the world through the Holy Spirit propels an ongoing, dynamic movement through history. Pope Benedict XVI enhanced this image of the church as a *communion* of believers journeying together toward a single, shared destination. Not long before becoming pontiff, he wrote that the phrase "expresses the historical nature of the pilgrim Church that will not be wholly herself until the paths of time have been traversed and have blossomed in the hands of God."[2]

For all Christians—not just Catholics—human mobility lends its language to the articulation of our identity. Once we perceive our lives of faith as a journey, we look toward human acts of migration with a new openness to what those experiences might tell us. Even a cursory review of teaching on migration from Judeo-Christian perspectives yields an astounding insight: those *without* a place hold a privileged place!

---

[2] Cardinal Joseph Ratzinger, *L'Osservatore Romano*, January 23, 2002.

Theologians and church leaders prefer the term *human mobility* when referring to migration in today's world. It reminds us that we are talking not only about a global phenomenon but also about people. Conceptually, it creates an inclusive term for different types of migratory experiences. Human mobility includes the desperate flight of refugees escaping to safety as well as the travels of economic refugees seeking opportunity.

*Migration* can take place within a country. United States schoolchildren learn about the movement of pioneers to the West. In a less-studied example, over five million African Americans moved from the rural South after the Second World War in the so-called Great Migration.

*Forced migration* describes being obliged to leave one's local place of origin. This usually results from poverty, warfare, and/or oppression. The displacement of Native Americans on the Trail of Tears is a shameful historical case. More recently, uprooted Iraqi families sought refuge after the Gulf War.

*Emigration* reflects leaving one's home country. Emigration comes before *immigration,* that is, entering a new nation with the hope of living and working there. Everywhere on the planet emigrants from *poor* countries seek entry into *well-off* countries.

As a survival strategy emigration benefits individual workers. It also extends a lifeline back to their sending communities. Figures from the World Bank report that emigrants working abroad send home hundreds of billions of dollars per year. Remittances rival formalized channels of development aid.

Refugee camps, populated by civilians affected by drought, famine, or conflict, shelter the most vulnerable members of our human family. Multiple sources on human mobility concur that women, children, and the elderly form the overwhelmingly majority of refugees displaced from their homes.

This sad reality is more prevalent than we realize. It may affect people we meet in our daily lives. Very early one Monday morning I sat on a bus next to a young woman with a suitcase. Twelve years ago, she told me, she and her family had left their native Liberia to escape civil unrest. They sought refuge in Sierra

Leone but had to flee again. From Ghana—where they lived in a camp for six years—they were accepted into a refugee program in Southern California. This grateful (but exhausted) young woman packed her suitcase every Sunday night. At dawn she set out, traveling two hours to work at a residence for handicapped adults. In her suitcase she carried textbooks. During her free time she took nursing classes at a community college.

Geographical displacement has been proven time and time again to be linked to sociopolitical and economic crisis. Migration is an indicator of detrimental factors at play in our increasingly globalized world. Human mobility points beyond itself toward the reasons *why* populations become uprooted in order to seek survival. Citizens are forced to emigrate when political violence endangers their well-being. Workers are drawn to new soil by the prospect of earning a decent living. Patterns of migration serve as indicators. They point to the roots of the problems that drive people into exile.

My brother, a lifelong member of the Catholic Worker movement,[3] ran a soup kitchen for several years. He once reflected on the prophetic role of the guests who came in from the street to eat: inner-city families unable to escape the cycle of welfare and unemployment; veterans wounded in body, mind, and spirit; the mentally ill, released from treatment centers only to become homeless. "They are our prophets," my brother explained. "They show us where our society is broken."

Blessed John Paul II emphasized that the "antidote" for illegal immigration is sustainable global development.[4] In world history our times are characterized by wildly disparate levels of quality of life. Half of the planet lives on less than two dollars a day, while a small percentage of the population enjoys unprecedented access to wealth. Sociologists document both the "push" factors that drive

---

[3] Started in 1933 by Dorothy Day and Peter Maurin, the movement embraces voluntary poverty, pacifism, and service through the works of mercy.

[4] He reiterated especially Pope Paul VI's *Populorum progressio* (1967). See also *Sollicitudo rei socialis* (1987), written for its twentieth anniversary, and *Ecclesia in America* (1999).

people from their homes and the "pull" factors that draw them to specific places. Workers (even highly skilled ones) from developing countries leave for better-paying jobs in developed ones. One religious sister from the Philippines told me of her brother, trained in medical school in their country. He earns more as a cabdriver in Chicago than as an underemployed doctor back home! Their country holds one of the highest *sending* rates for migrants and one of the lowest *receiving* rates for immigrants.

Intensified interconnections among countries is another sign of the times. Make no mistake, global exchange is nothing new. Who can imagine Italy without pasta and tomato sauce? Ireland without potatoes? England without black tea? However, inconceivable as the thought may be, these culinary innovations were introduced in past centuries through international trade. Potatoes and tomatoes are native to the Americas, while pasta and black tea are attributed to Asia.

As if following the same trajectory but at a much quicker speed, global interaction has accelerated in our time. By the time I finish breakfast, I will have enjoyed products owing their existence to *several* continents. Today, my morning cup of coffee comes from beans harvested in Africa, roasted in Europe, grown with seeds and fertilizers from the United States. Political concessions and economic trade agreements formed a long and complicated chain of procedures to bring this cup of coffee to my table. If I were to investigate the rest of my breakfast, chances are that the other items on my table would have followed the same pattern. Foods are cultivated, processed, packaged, marketed, and sold across numerous borders. International trade and migration are not new. What's *new* is the intensity and the scope of far-reaching effects of globalization on local cultures and economies.

In the heat of the controversies—and, around the planet, immigration is controversial—Christians are enjoined not to forget the human aspect of migration. Formed and *in*formed by scripture and tradition, we often see that the realities lived by migrants do not coincide with what we understand as God's plan for us. In particular, the indignities to which refugees and trafficked migrants are subjected contradict universally recognized human rights.

Religious leaders who address human mobility from within their faith traditions echo the biblical prophets who, in the words of the great Jewish scholar Abraham Heschel, attempted to bring the world into divine focus.

Once the lens through which we regard migrants is changed, our perceptions will change as well. Debates on immigration pose the legitimate concern of whether newcomers are a "drain" on economies, but they rarely consider the positive contributions (monetary or otherwise) that these same arrivals make to their receiving communities.

The US Chamber of Commerce website refutes myths about immigrant workers. Contrary to stereotype, it insists, they complement the native-born workforce and pay taxes that support local, state, and national economies. They use social services disproportionately less while contributing more to the country's safety nets. They produce a positive impact on the labor market and even create new jobs!

Of course, migrants are not statistics; they are people. And like all human beings, they possess rights and responsibilities, and they are capable of becoming integral members of their host communities. Immigrants tend to bring with them optimism, energy, inventiveness, and the drive to establish themselves in their adopted countries. Even those who remain "on the fringe" offer something. Temporary workers on guest-worker visas proffer their labor. Migrants en route to another destination present the opportunity to grow in solidarity, awareness, and hospitality.

Writing during the time that Europe struggled to absorb the horrors of the Holocaust, German theologian Johann Baptist Metz articulated a spirituality he called "a mysticism of open eyes": "It is a mysticism that especially makes visible all invisible and inconvenient suffering, and—convenient or not—pays attention to it and takes responsibility for it, for the sake of a God who is a friend to human beings."[5]

---

[5] Johann Baptist Metz, *A Passion for God: The Mystical-Political Dimension of Christianity*, trans. J. Matthew Ashley (Mahweh, NJ: Paulist Press, 1998), 163

The suffering of undocumented migrants, in particular, eludes the public eye. Rendered invisible, they live and work in a perpetual borderland, displaced from their countries of origin yet unacknowledged in their new settings. Largely unprotected by their host countries' provisions and laws, they are vulnerable to the worst abuses. Advocates often point to public policies that "scapegoat" immigrants—while societies as a whole profit from their labor.

Even more disturbing is the plight of victims of human trafficking. International organizations estimate that, around the globe, an untold number of people are coerced into forced labor, including sexual exploitation. Whatever the statistics—any number is too high.

*The Church in the Modern World* (1965) from Vatican II states:

> Justice and equity . . . require that the mobility, which is necessary in a developing economy . . . be regulated . . . [to] keep the life of individuals and their families from becoming insecure and precarious. When workers come from another country or district . . . all discrimination in wages and working conditions must be carefully avoided. . . . All the people, moreover, above all the public authorities, must treat them not as mere tools of production but as persons, and must help them to bring their families to live with them. . . . They must see to it that these works are incorporated into the social life of the country or region which receives them. (no. 66)

Not only in the United States but also in other corners of the globe where desperate newcomers arrive in search of work, political discourse can stagnate. Opposing sides are overwhelmed by myriad issues. Long-lasting, equitable policies are more nuanced than easy answers will allow. So many aspects must be taken into account, and so many parties are involved—each with its own legitimate concerns. Concern for migrants is not convenient!

Superficial discourse is interrupted by the urgent need to address uncomfortable questions. With global inequity at historic levels, how can we prevent families from emigrating? What are the responsibilities of receiving countries? What are reasonable limits, and how should they be enforced? Is it fair to accept new residents when a country's own people face unemployment? The list could go on and on.

And there are no easy answers.

Let me give an example. The leaders of religious bodies in the United States explicitly uphold the right of sovereign nations to control their borders. This issue is not disputed. At the same time, many faith-based entities look at the growing violence and desperation along the US-Mexico border as a human rights crisis. Efforts are led by ecumenical groups to supply water and first-aid kits at emergency stations in the desert. The two positions are not meant to be exclusive but complementary. A joint pastoral letter on migration, *Strangers No Longer: Together on the Journey of Hope,* was issued by the US and Mexican bishops in 2003. Its vision reconciles these seemingly irreconcilable differences.

To paraphrase Metz, this invisible and inconvenient suffering calls out for attention. His quotation can be taken a step further. We know that God is "a friend to human beings" because God *became* a human being. Surely a God who migrated from heaven to be born to a refugee family—to belong to a people painfully and intimately versed in Exodus and exile journeys—surely this God would ask us to look for his presence among migrants. Jesus was a migrant. How could migrants *not* matter?

It is my hope that this reflection on why migrants matter will enliven our commitment as Christians to look for the image of Christ in our sisters and brothers—even when his face is difficult to see. Church teaching on human mobility is the gift of centuries of reflection on sacred scriptures; pastoral accompaniment of peoples and individuals who migrate; and the experience of being a people on pilgrimage. It is a revelation of God's love, which asks for our own decision to love in return.

In the Hebrew Bible we are charged with the duty to love our neighbors, an injunction upheld and enlarged by Jesus in the Great Commandment (Mk 12:28–34; cf. Mt 19:19; Jn 13:34). My purpose for writing these reflections is to quicken our *desire* to glimpse the face of the Lord in the lives of migrants. For what love is not born of desire?

The editing of this book coincides with a prophetic act by Pope Francis. On his first apostolic trip outside Rome, the pope visited the rocky, desolate Sicilian island of Lampedusa. This way station for emigrants recently saw a particularly deadly incident in which a dozen Africans lost their lives. Tens of thousands of migrants and asylum seekers have passed through Lampedusa over the years. Fleeing poverty and conflict, they attempt to reach European shores. Men, women, and children are crammed onto unsafe vessels, exposed to the elements in their desperate bid for a better life.

Pope Francis thanked the residents of the island not only for coming out to greet him, but also for their patience. He acknowledged how difficult it has become to live normal lives in their hometown. Boarding a Coastal Guard patrol ship, he recognized the necessary work of those who enforce the law and provide security in the waters. His primary (though by no means exclusive) concern, however, was for the most vulnerable: migrants whose lives are endangered.

The pope cast a wreath into the water to mourn the deaths at Lampedusa and at other sites where migrants have died. He wore purple—the color of repentance—to atone for the world's "globalization of indifference" to migrants' plight. For the simple mass, an altar and lectern were fashioned out of wood salvaged from the island's "boat cemetery." A ship hull—painted in vivid red, blue, green, and yellow—held up a tabletop covered by a white altar cloth.

This brave, bright little boat had transported migrants who risked their lives. Tossed about on choppy waters, it had been battered by adverse waves and overloaded with the weight of humanity. The symbol could not have been more apt. The migrant boat that had carried the body of Christ in the person of migrants now carried the body of Christ in the Eucharist.

For Christians, an altar—traditionally made of wood—recalls the cross. The migrant boat reminds us of Jesus' crucifixion, personified in the travails of refugees and asylum seekers. Like the cross, it also signifies Resurrection. Crossing over can lead to new life.

Human mobility certainly entails sacrifice. Migration has caused—and been caused by—tremendous suffering.

It has also served as a source of great blessing.

Chapter Two

# From Exile
# to Exodus

Above my desk hangs a picture of the flight into Egypt. Painted on papyrus, this image made by Coptic Christians shows the Holy Family fleeing into an uncertain future.

An elderly Joseph with flowing silver beard carries a staff and a meager bundle of belongings. He looks ahead, sandals sturdy, posture resolute. Above him, an angel leads the way. One arm shows the path, and the other arm directs our attention to the figures below.

Mary sits astride a gray donkey. She gazes directly at the viewer, as does the infant Jesus—wrapped in swaddling clothes—in her arms. Settled peacefully on the donkey's back, the almond-shaped eyes of mother and child look gently back at the viewer in contemplative silence. Mary's circular red robe enfolds them both. Emerald green plants line the path, and bronze sand shines under their feet. They are poor refugees, but each member of the Holy Family wears a brilliant golden halo. Head bowed, the donkey trudges along the road toward safety.

Throughout the gospel texts the evangelists presuppose an intimate familiarity with Jewish migration narratives on the part of their readers. It is simply not possible to talk about Jesus Christ without taking into account these great journeys—which, early Christians believed, God *lived* in his very person. In Fr. Daniel Groody's words, Jesus is the quintessential migrant. God migrated from heaven to earth, taking on our humanity, and died on the cross in order to return us from exile to our true home.[1]

## BEGINNINGS

Before the dawn of historical memory, the Book of Genesis is already shaped by migrations. The legend of the Fall culminates in Adam and Eve being cast out of the Garden of Eden. Our first parents are forced into exile. Thus begin biblical ruminations on the human condition based on experiences of migration. These narratives will extend over millennia.

The overarching image of migration as spiritual journey continues in the figure of Abraham. Entering into a singular relationship with God, he is recognized as the father of the three great monotheistic religions. Before being renamed as a sign of his new identity, Abram received a calling. Told to leave his land, his kin, and his father's house, he set out for a land that, God promised, "I will show you." His faith was expressed by being willing to undertake a journey.

In the ancient world nomadic peoples regularly traveled; however, leaving one's kin and father's house behind meant turning one's back on the clan. Abraham and those who went with him gave up more than the familiarity of their homes. They traded the security of their tribe for a precarious pilgrimage. They exchanged the normative polytheistic religion for a novel belief in One True God.

Many immigrants set out from their homelands in search of freedom. Perhaps Abraham would never have been free to worship the One True God without emigrating. Leaving one's land can also mean seeking new forms of civic and political engagement.

In a down-to-earth interpretation, emigration entails abandoning the natural setting, as well. Physical landscapes may remain imprinted on emigrants' minds and souls. To give a personal

---

[1] Daniel Groody, CSC, "A Theology of Migration," *America* (February 7, 2011).

example, until I returned to the panorama of my childhood, I hungered to glimpse a certain, exact proportion of river to mountains and sky. God's pledge to Abraham meant that his descendants would eventually settle into the landscape of the Promised Land.

And so . . . salvation history begins with one person's decision to migrate, aptly expressed in the Spanish phrase *amar a Dios en tierra ajena*—to love God in a foreign land.

## THE JOSEPH CYCLE

At a Human Mobility Conference in Mexico I once participated in a reflection on Joseph and his brothers in Genesis from the perspective of migration. The stories in this cycle, originally passed along through oral tradition, began to be written down during the Exile and the return to Jerusalem.

The lengthy narrative of Jacob's twelve sons sounds startling familiar to modern ears. The saga opens with a scene of human trafficking! Slave labor sets the plot, reminding me of a disgraceful chapter in our own country's history. Unjust detention lands Joseph in the loneliest of places: prison in a foreign country.

Once Joseph is freed and successfully established as a resident alien, the story takes a surprising turn. Their own land decimated by a famine, his brothers travel to Egypt as economic refugees. Joseph's desire to see his young brother Benjamin with his own eyes after years of estrangement is similar to many contemporary situations. Having assimilated remarkably well into Egyptian culture (though not fully into Egyptian religion), Joseph extends a lifeline to the other members of his family, just as immigrants do today.

The redactors of the Joseph cycle were acquainted with the need to balance integration into a host culture with the preservation of religious identity. They themselves were living through the Babylonian Exile. In the text these issues would come to the fore as the Jewish people settle in the Promised Land. As a people set apart, they nevertheless had to learn to live alongside their neighbors. But first comes the Exodus: the rite of passage that charts the course for biblical spirituality.

## EXODUS

Each year my husband and I prepare a simple Seder meal for our children. We remind them that the night his passion began, Jesus shared this meal, a Jewish celebration, with his followers.

The children watch curiously as we set aside special items beforehand. (They are not as interested in the thorough house-cleaning that also takes place.) I put out my grandmother's table-cloth and set the table with our best plates and wine glasses. Our annual dinner includes foods that allow a retelling of the Exodus story. Apples mixed with nuts and cinnamon represent mortar and bricks. Salt water tells of the tears and sweat of slavery, as do bitter herbs. The ten drops of grape juice dripped lightly from our fingertips onto our plates remind us of the ten plagues. The cup of our joy is lessened by the suffering (even the just punishment) of our enemies.

As Christians, the symbols of the Seder take on an added dimension. The wine's burgundy color leaps to our eyes, reminding us of the Blood shed for us. The matzoh ignites our imagination as we think of how Christ partook of unleavened bread at the last supper. A hard-boiled egg and fresh vegetables promise the coming of spring—and of resurrection. The main course symbolizes the sacrifice of the Lamb, the one who gave his Body so that his followers can "pass over" into new life.

It would be impossible to reconstruct in detail the Seder as practiced in the first century, but we do know that it was widely observed. I imagine Jesus as a child, celebrating with Joseph and Mary, asking, "Why is this night different from all others?" I picture Jesus as an adolescent and as a young man, singing the psalms that traditionally follow the meal. These images help me to place Jesus in his own religious and cultural context, which then allows me to enter the gospel more deeply.

The covenant was foreshadowed in the exile of Adam and Eve. It was promised to Abraham, our migrant father in faith. Jacob's sons—one victim of human trafficking and eleven economic refugees—inherited the legacy. At first, living as resident aliens, the Hebrews were enslaved in a foreign land. Freedom came when they emigrated. The covenant was finally established in the most unlikely of places, a desert borderland.

God did not initiate a divine alliance with the people once they were settled. God chose them while they were migrants! Displaced, uprooted, homeless, often unfaithful and disoriented—God called them onward. Traveling by providence alone, they learned to trust in the Lord and freely to embrace the relationship offered to them. Migrant steps in the desert trace the paradigm of biblical spirituality.

Time and time again the Lord of the Hebrew Bible enjoins the Chosen People to remember that they were once slaves whom God set free. They are sojourners who were led home to the Promised Land. The commandments themselves are founded in this relationship of God to the people, "I am the Lord your God, who brought you out of the land of Egypt, out of the house of slavery" (Ex 20:2). It is how God tells the people who God is.

It also forms the basis for who the people are. Biblical authors return again and again to this fundamental aspect of their identity (e.g., Ex 22:21; Dt 24:17; Lv 19:33–34). The Book of Deuteronomy includes this divinely inspired instruction: "You shall also love the stranger, for you were strangers in the land of Egypt" (10:19). The prophetic writings follow the same trajectory. When the prophets reproach the tribes and their leaders for neglecting the poor, they specify mistreatment of resident aliens (e.g., Jer 7:6; Ezek 22:29; Mal 3:51). Compassion toward foreigners is tied directly to what it means to live as God's people.

We believers today place ourselves in this line, which threads through history into the present day. Our identity hinges on the fact that we, too, were once slaves—but now are free. We, too, wandered in a desert—until we came home (for Christians, in Christ). And until we arrive at our final destination, we are all, still, on a journey. In this light, remembering that we are *all* migrants and immigrants is fundamental to biblical spirituality. It tells us who we are.

## EXILE

Perhaps the chapter most neglected by Christians in our reading of biblical spirituality is the period of the Exile.

Scholars point to this era as the beginning of the Jewish Diaspora. Christians are markedly unaware of its importance in Jewish history and consequently, for the early church (and the writers who redacted the New Testament). Themes that arise from this chapter of history seem particularly relevant in today's world.

When the Babylonian Empire conquered the Southern Kingdom, it laid waste to Jerusalem and the surrounding areas. The Temple was pillaged. The young, the educated, and the influential were forcibly taken. Not only was the land ravaged, but those citizens most likely to rebuild the wounded country were targeted. Waves of *deportations* took place—unfortunately, another familiar word. More people have been deported from the United States in the past ten years than in the previous one hundred years combined.

On occasion I have discussed with immigrant groups their reflections on the Exodus and the Exile. When asked which biblical episode more closely reflects their own experience, at first the members of the group unanimously respond, "the Exodus." Full of vigor and optimism, the group members had emigrated from impoverished settings that provided little or no work, liberated from oppressive societies or corrupt governments. They made their way to the "promised land," ready to work and eager to seek a better life for their families. Often, emigrants are the "best and brightest"—the workers or students who find the courage to leave when their potential will not be realized at home. They brave borders at great risk, submitting to the dangers and indignities that may befall them.

Yet, as discussions continued and parents began to talk about the realities of raising their children in their adopted country, the subject of exile inevitably arose. Recently arrived immigrants were just realizing how hard adaptation would be. Some were not able to find fulfilling work (for example, a former worker in

her country's health ministry now packs boxes in a
exhilaration of arriving in the "land flowing with mi
had become mixed with other feelings. Perhaps for t
lives they would perform jobs for which native-born peop.. ...
not even consider applying.

Homesickness can be exacerbated when going back home for a
visit is out of the question. New immigrants, especially, expressed
the fear that leaving the United States would jeopardize their immigration status. If they are awaiting residency, their movement
is restricted. If they are undocumented, they may leave—but how
would they come back? The sense of exile becomes acute. The
death of a parent or loved one often brings on an intensified an-
guish, compounded by other emotions such as guilt. Even joyous
events like weddings, graduations, patronal feasts, and birthdays
provoke ambivalent reactions when an emigrant cannot be there
to participate.

For those who had begun to settle into their lives as new
Americans, foremost among their comments was concern for
their children.

On the one hand, the parents in my groups were proud that
their children were able to assimilate so easily. (I had the same
incredulous reaction when my husband and I lived in Mexico
and our children quickly surpassed us in language and in cultural
competence.) On the other hand, they feared their children might
take on aspects of the new culture that would conflict with their
way of life. The distance between their own and their children's
levels of acculturation might cause a vacuum—one that might be
filled by the worst of both worlds.

At times a burden of grief—a sense of loss beyond simple nostalgia—hides underneath day-to-day life. Psychologists have even
come up with a name for it: migratory mourning. The families in
my groups expressed a sense of melancholy. One father explained:

> "My boys have never seen my village, have never met my
> parents, and have never eaten food from our farm. Yet here
> they have the chance for a better life. How can I say I'm not
> happy? They have the opportunities I never had. I haven't

been back (and I can't go back). It's not that I regret it . . .
but I can't find the words to explain to them how much this
costs me and their mother. It may sound strange, but for me,
what hurts me the most is that they don't have any idea what
they are missing."

The most pressing necessity, that of adaptation to one's surroundings, means that these deeper feelings may be neglected and
can cause depression or hopelessness; when channeled, however,
they can lead to intense spiritual growth and creativity. Movement
beyond borders opens more than simply physical space: it provides
new terrain for the soul. Experiences of displacement can stimulate
great art and literature, an impulse realized even more fully by the
next generation.

Like the immigrant members of my groups, the families of the
Babylonian Exile—traumatized by the destruction of the Temple and
the conquest of their homeland—found meaning in their faith. The
exilic psalms (written and sung during the Babylonian Exile) pour
out feelings of homesickness, impotence, nostalgia, and despair.
Beloved to peoples who have gone through their own upheavals,
Psalm 137 gives eloquent expression to migratory mourning:

> By the rivers of Babylon—
>     there we sat down and there we wept
>     when we remembered Zion.
> On the willows there
>     we hung up our harps.
> For there our captors
>     asked us for songs,
> and our tormentors asked for mirth, saying,
>     "Sing us one of the songs of Zion!"
>
> How could we sing the LORD's song
>     in a foreign land?
> If I forget you, O Jerusalem,
>     let my right hand wither! (1–5)

In addition to creating new psalms, religious leaders began to redact existing sacred writings into a form future generations could inherit as their legacy. Oral traditions were written down, probably for the first time. The original Exile—that of our first parents, Adam and Eve—was recalled. The migrations of Abraham and Sarah, Lot and his family, Hagar and Ishmael, fold into the stories of Isaac and Rebecca and their sons, culminating in the Twelve Tribes emigrating to Egypt. From then, the Exodus story dominates religious memory. The people of God in Exile found themselves on the same path, traveling along the same journey of faith. They might not have the Temple, and they might live in captivity far from the Promised Land, but the word of God would lead them home.

The post-exilic psalms rejoice in the return of Jews to the Promised Land. We also know, of course, that not all families did, in fact, return; the Jewish Diaspora had begun. While exact numbers cannot be determined, a significant number of Jews remained outside their home country—spreading throughout the ancient world to form communities where the word of God took central place in their lives and worship.

A compendium of sacred texts produced as divinely inspired writings, the Hebrew Bible returns again and again to those great stories of journeys that formed Jewish consciousness. Scholars now debate the historicity of epic figures such as Abraham and Moses, but could the Bible have been written without living (historical) people of ancient times having undergone episodes of actual geographical migration? The unequivocal answer is no.

Could Christianity have spread throughout the Ancient World without migration? Again the unequivocal answer is no. We know from the Gospels, the Acts of the Apostles, and the epistles that Diaspora Jews returning to Jerusalem during the holy days heard the gospel message. We learn that the early church took root throughout the Roman Empire thanks to these widespread Jewish communities. Itinerant missionaries took up our Lord's commission to carry the good news to the world.

## JESUS, THE MESSIAH

As a Jew, Jesus' own religious formation was shaped by biblical spirituality, notably, the Exodus and the Exile. His first followers understood that his incarnation, ministry, death, and resurrection encompassed and embodied these events—in cosmic proportion. When the evangelists presented Jesus as the Messiah, they confessed him as the divine fulfillment of these epic stories. In his very person Christ relives the normative chapters of the history of his people.

Jesus draws upon the repertoire of salvation history to reveal the reign of God. Steeped in religious symbols his teaching does not empty but rather renews their meaning. Two thousand years removed from these symbols, we tend to lose their depth of association. Portrayal of Jesus as the new Moses . . . echoes of the Exodus in the infancy narratives . . . the Suffering Servant of the Exile . . . the paschal mystery as a *passing over* . . . the vision of the New Jerusalem, where Diaspora communities come home—all these images depend upon familiarity with the biblical spirituality of migration.

Saint Luke tells us that while Jesus was still in Mary's womb—before he was even born—he already traveled. His mother's immediate response to the angel Gabriel's news was to journey "with haste" to the hill country of Judea (1:39).

Mary returns home after a three-month visit to her cousin Elizabeth (echoing an account of the Ark of the Covenant in 2 Sm 6). No sooner does Mary return to Nazareth than she sets out again, this time with Joseph, on the journey to Bethlehem. Obliged by governmental policy, the couple is forced to disregard the health and safety of mother and unborn child. A census is being carried out for the most unpopular of reasons: taxation. While not expecting to benefit from this decree (in fact, it might even further impoverish them), the couple must comply.

Mary and Joseph are presented by Saint Luke as vulnerable migrants in need of shelter and hospitality. Our Lord is born far from home, on a journey. This image of Christ brings strength and consolation to us on our own travels. Whether or not we have crossed geographical borders . . . whether or not we have strayed far from home . . . Jesus understands us. He witnesses our migratory mourning, while at the same time, he propels us along the path toward new life.

In the reflection groups I shared with immigrants, participants identified with Jesus even in their moments of most dire need. One Cuban asylum seeker who had sailed miles of ocean expressed succinctly, "When my water ran out, I remembered how he said, 'I thirst.' I knew that even in my terrible thirst, his love for me would never be quenched." Believers find in Christ the companion for our life journeys, journeys that become grafted onto his.

Saint Matthew provides another perspective on human mobility in the infancy narratives. He does not allow us to bask for long in the glowing scene where the Wise Men offer their gifts; he turns our gaze, instead, to a startling episode of displacement, uncertainty, and terror. In a reversal of the Exodus story, Mary and Joseph set out with the infant Jesus for Egypt. They do not know where they will receive hospitality or how they will make a living. A wave of politically motivated violence (recalling Pharaoh's murder of Hebrew newborns) makes the message clear. The Holy Family is depicted not only as migrants, but also as refugees.

Modern-day readers concerned with factuality may inquire whether there is historical evidence for this passage, known in tradition as the flight into Egypt. A better question might be why Saint Matthew chose to include this text in his Gospel? And why has it become beloved in all lands throughout the centuries (evidenced by the Coptic painting above my desk)? Similarly, we might wonder about the exact details of Saint Luke's census.

But wouldn't that make us miss the point? Mary (the new Ark of the Covenant) travels toward the destination of fulfillment. Jesus' birth takes place in the hometown of King David, and God's long-promised Firstborn comes to us. Christ is laid in a manger, a place of nourishment for the flocks. A new covenant is made along a journey . . . much as the original covenant was established with God's people as they wandered in a desert.

Jesus' ministry throughout Galilee reinforces the biblical image of the Exodus. Instead of establishing himself in one particular village or town, Christ retraced the steps of God's people in the desert. His itinerant mission opens with a painful beginning.

After the Holy Spirit drives him to the desert, where he spends forty days—recalling the years of Exodus—Jesus begins to teach in the synagogues of Galilee. He returns to Nazareth, the town where he grew up. In his home synagogue, he announces the fulfillment of the reign of God, reading from the scroll of the prophet Isaiah. The words prove too much for his fellow villagers. They had known him since childhood. His relatives lived among them, ordinary people like everyone else. How dare he? They drive him out of town—and would have even cast him over a cliff. In this rural setting—where one's clan determined livelihood, marriage prospects, social status, and wealth—Jesus is homeless (Lk 4:16–30).

Saint Mark and Saint Matthew present a softer picture of Jesus' return to Nazareth. Their versions do not include the mob scene that Saint Luke so vividly portrays. These gospels do concur in depicting the lack of faith on the part of the villagers. Jesus cannot work miracles because of their "unbelief" (Mt 13:54–58; Mk 6:1–6). The ministry of Jesus would not be based on a tribal identity. Even the members of his own family cannot claim preferences based on belonging to his clan (Lk 8:19–21; Mt 12:46–50; Mk 3:31–35). To join this new family, believers first had to disengage from the privileges conferred by kinship. They had to leave behind false security and exclusivity, becoming, in a real sense, migrants.

The Hebrews, wandering for forty years, were tested in the desert. After Jesus' baptism the Holy Spirit drove him into the desert to be tempted. When Jesus retires to a secluded place to pray, evangelists recall the Exodus journey, a time of being tested in faith . . . of moving toward freedom . . . and of seeking communion with the One True God, whom Jesus called Abba. The relationship is nurtured in desert prayer.

The Lord commissions his disciples to follow his example. Like him, they go from town to town to preach and to heal. Sending them out in pairs, Jesus instructs them to travel as migrants. Carrying few or no possessions, they are to depend on the hospitality of those who receive them (Mt 10:1–15; Mk 6:8–11; Lk 9:1–5; 10:1–12). The twelve disciples resemble the twelve tribes, and the seventy disciples recall the seventy elders of the Exodus.

Saint Matthew quotes Jesus as saying, "Foxes have holes, and birds of the air have nests; but the Son of Man has nowhere to lay his head" (8:20). In the sacred scriptures Jesus himself is the Way (Jn 14:6). Being at home with Christ does not mean setting up residence in any one, particular place. Being at home with Jesus means coming to the Father. Being at home with him means living in the reign of God.

Jesus embraces the Father in total freedom. In the final stages of his public ministry, Jesus undertakes the journey to Jerusalem, becoming the Passover Lamb, who sets us free, as well.

Christ chose to live in the Exodus . . . so that he could rescue *us* from exile.

## A PILGRIM CHURCH

During his public ministry Jesus sent out his disciples to outlying areas; after the resurrection he sends them out to the whole world. Saint Matthew ends his Gospel with the Great Commission. The risen Christ tells the disciples, "Go therefore and make disciples of all nations" (28:19). In the words of the Book of Revelation, the word of God would extend to people of "every nation, from all tribes and people of languages" (7:9).

Evangelization was made possible through the network of Jewish synagogues spread throughout the Diaspora. Saint Paul and the other epistle writers often described themselves as sojourners or pilgrims—a literal designation, given their missionary travels. They encouraged other Christians to perceive themselves in this light, as well. Although living as settled inhabitants of established communities, their conversion, nevertheless, called for a spiritual migration, a crossing of boundaries.

During Christianity's first years non-Jews first had to enter biblical spirituality. Christian Jews had to welcome Gentiles into "their territory," the covenant. Both Jews and non-Jews had to traverse social, religious, and political norms as fellow Christians. Together, believers learned to see themselves as a single people set apart for the sake of the gospel. In the Letter to the Galatians, Saint Paul writes, "There is no longer Jew or Greek, there is no longer slave or free, there is no longer male and female; for all of you are one in Christ Jesus" (3:28).

The writer of the First Letter of Saint Peter admonishes Christians to live exemplary lives as "aliens and exiles" (1:11). Religious minorities in the wider Ancient World, they are inserted among nonbelievers. Saint Paul uses similar language to relay another message. He employs terms of citizenship and belonging in the Letter to the Ephesians. To use contemporary language, for Saint Paul there are no "illegals" in the reign of God. Members of the believing community "are no longer strangers and aliens, but . . . citizens with the saints and also members of the household of God" (2:19).

✦ ✦ ✦

Today, Christians still find metaphors that express our spiritual reality in the biblical language of migration. If our first parents were pushed from the Garden of Eden into exile, our life in Christ restores us to our true home. Our exile turns into exodus: a pilgrimage of salvation.

Biblical spirituality teaches that we are citizens, together, in the reign of God. Doesn't this mean in a sense that we are resident aliens in our respective countries? Until our communities fully reflect gospel values, and until we arrive before the throne of the Lamb, our true destination is not yet realized. Loving our families, serving our local communities, and making our nations strong and safe do not conflict with this identity. They put it into practice.

In one of my reflection groups a young immigrant summed up: "I may never go back to my country, but I will do my very best to be a good American. And I will never forget that I am on my way to my true home."

# Chapter Three

# The Great Hunger

Every day when I drop off and pick up my children from school, we pass a stone cross. In Celtic style, a ring encircles its intersection. Its full curves embrace the unbent cruciform. Carved into solid granite, the cross stands in perfect proportion. Eternal, aesthetically pleasing, it is solid as the rock from which it is formed.

From a sideways vantage, the round flow and outstretched arms are not visible. Approaching from the east, I see instead a sliver of stone, a granite splinter. The cross looks like a raised ashen finger poking the sky. Coming full-front to its stone face, I take in the circular sweep of its ring, a symbol of infinity. Untiringly rigid, it is both heavy and beautiful.

On closer inspection the stone cross reveals the motive for its existence. The heart of its polished gray surface is chiseled with flowing patterns. Words and images beckon me closer. The lower portion of the granite mass is inscribed:

> 1845–1852
> *An Gorta Mor*
> The Great Hunger

If not for the pictures that accompany its words, I might have escaped being confronted by the cross's dedication: "In memory of the souls who perished during the Great Hunger in Ireland." But three rectangles stacked one on top of the other frame images impossible to ignore. They portray scenes that were lived out by millions of Irish people, including my forebears.

The first is titled "Starvation." It shows a man's body, dressed in clothes with frayed hems, being led away in a horse-drawn cart. The driver's whip lingers ominously in the air. A woman with downturned mouth looks on, two small children clinging to her tattered skirts.

The second small frame reads "Eviction." Thatched huts are etched into the background. A man in peasant garb—hands folded in a gesture of supplication—pleads with two soldiers. But a simple table and chair, already turned out of the house and tossed carelessly to the ground, give evidence that no mercy will be given.

A third and final image completes the unholy triad. This last frame is almost too painful to look upon. Titled "Emigration," it portrays a ship with full sails setting out on the ocean. The ship's prow points away from the shore, where onlookers huddle in miserable farewell. Some wave goodbye. Other simply watch. An older woman has sunk to her knees on the ground, burying her face in her hands. Another woman holds a baby in her arms and shelters two crying children. A young boy buries his face in an old man's chest. A century and a half ago this could have been my ancestors' emigration.

In my mission work I have encountered the same three stark realities that are etched into the granite cross.

*Starvation.* My parents and brother ran urban soup kitchens. Street people—wracked by drugs and alcohol, reeling from the multiple traumas of their lives—might eat their only meal of the day there. Not the same as lack of food in refugee camps, certainly, but hunger nevertheless.

*Eviction.* My first experiences in the developing world took place in a rank shanty town with open sewage. Rural people displaced from their lands built makeshift shelters along railroad tracks. Eviction by armed police was a constant threat to these squatters, who had already been forced from their farms.

*Emigration.* Helping new Americans to make a home in our great nation—the land of opportunity—is dear to my heart.

So how is it that I had never looked at my own history through these same three lenses?

The cross works curious effects on me. It makes me proud to have my ethnic heritage prominently and artistically honored; at the same time it makes me uncomfortable. The first time I studied the images on its smooth plane, I realized how very little I knew about where my people had come from. The granite cross became for me an intrusion on my conscience, a splinter under the skin. It weighed on my thoughts—evidence of an old, forgotten wound.

Irish and Irish American writers describe a national trauma whose pain has lessened over time but that still marks those who inherit it. My task seems to come from an entirely opposite direction. Far from being able to sketch the ways in which my family had interiorized the Great Hunger, I returned again and again to a proverbial blank canvas. Of course, in school I had been exposed to the so-called Irish potato famine. And I now realize that my grandmother had done her best to instill a sense of family history into my mother, my brother, and me. But in just two generations we seemed to have developed an impenetrable skin. The wound had grown over. How is it that I have arrived at middle age in the United States of America—a country of immigrants—impervious to my great-grandparents' history? I asked my family about this cultural amnesia from which I found myself waking.

The granite cross made me realize that until now, starvation, eviction, and migration existed for me outside of my kinship boundaries. I had never recognized them as intruding upon my own lineage. Perhaps in pragmatic American fashion, my sense of family extends only as far back as those ancestors whom I remember. Or perhaps—the more likely explanation—in this country of immigrants, our longing to remember is overshadowed by our desire to forget.

Whatever the case, I owned nothing of this collective memory except for two slivers, two shards.

Here is what I do remember.

When telling us about our family history, my Irish American grandmother repeated two refrains. Neither made any sense to me, but both seemed to hold huge significance for her. The first barely made any impact on my young ears: "We are from County Mayo." Unfamiliar with Irish geography, I paid little attention to the mention of a foreign location.

The second shard of memory, which I am sorry to report made even less of an impression, was, "You have ancestors who fought in the Civil War." Again, this phrase seemed to hold great significance for my grandmother, though I had no idea of its meaning beyond the simple statement of a not-very-noteworthy fact.

Since my grandmother is now gone, I turned to the person who lovingly and carefully used to remove my splinters, my mother. In her kitchen she recounted bits and pieces of stories.

My great-great-grandfather, James, came from County Mayo to work on the Erie Canal. A relative had sent word from America of the plentiful jobs to be had. The canal builders would employ immigrants for the backbreaking labor required.

At the time of their decision the family was going through a brief episode that, tragically, would turn out to be only a harbinger of much worse to come. In past centuries the traditional diet was based on dairy products and grain. But the potato had taken over as the food staple of the population, especially the poor. A bad potato crop that year meant that James, his wife, Brigid, and their children would go hungry. When their crops failed, it was a precursor to the more devastating blight a decade later.

In County Mayo (as in other areas) rural laborers lived on farm sublets, dependent on absentee landowners for whom they raised export crops and livestock. The effects of the Penal Laws were still being felt. Under them, Irish Catholics had been prohibited from owning land, voting, holding political office, entering a profession, and even speaking their native language or practicing their religion. When tenant farmers or cottiers could not meet their rents, landlords were entitled by law to throw male heads of household into jail. In County Mayo, a single English landowner held deed to sixty thousand acres of land. Reputed to be one of the most punitive landlords, he approved scores of evictions carried out on his property during the Great Hunger.

James and his brothers could not have imagined the extent to which Ireland would be wounded by the Great Hunger. They could not have imagined, either, the hemorrhaging of its population. Emigration had been part of Irish history for as long as anyone could remember; what would change was its sheer magnitude. Their surname was known in County Mayo for its number of vocations to the priesthood (my grandmother's people referred to a certain cemetery as "*our* priests' graveyard," it was so densely populated with family clergymen). But soon their family would be known for something else, namely, casting a lifeline to other relatives.

The canal built, James established himself in Cleveland, Ohio, after marrying a young woman from Canada. James and Helen had no sooner started a family than they began to receive desperate pleas for help from James's Irish compatriots.

In the mid-1800s an airborne fungus transported by ships from the Americas infected the potato crops of Ireland. A nauseating stench spread as blackened potato plants rotted in the fields. In an astonishingly short time whole areas were deprived of their most important food staple. Desperate families, evicted from their lands, wandered the roads, dying of "road fever"—a catch-all designation for cholera, dysentery, smallpox, and influenza. The exact number of deaths could not be calculated, given the loss of entire families swept away by starvation or emigration, but it may have been a million or more. County Mayo was one of the worst affected.

The term *Irish Potato Famine* does not accurately describe this fateful period. More aptly it has been called the Great Hunger. While the potato crop was lost, other food sources were not. The export of meat, for example, actually increased during these same years. Many factors of poverty combined to create a nightmarish situation (dependence on only one crop, tenant farming, inadequate health services, and more). Lack of early and effective intervention on the part of the British government cemented the disaster.

For many families, leaving their homeland became the only way to survive. In an unthinkably short period of time Ireland lost one-fourth of its population to emigration, starvation, and disease. Emigrants like my great-great grandfather James used their wages in order to send for family members devastated by the Great Hunger. Women came as well as men, in the same numbers, to work as domestics or factory workers.

The first generation of Irish Americans raised on American soil inherited an intense and complicated relationship to their parents' native land. An elderly friend tells of growing up in an Irish enclave in the Bronx during the first decades of twentieth century. In all the years of his childhood, he recounts, there was one word that was ever present but rarely spoken. The word was *Ireland*. It was never pronounced, he mused, because it was referred to instead simply as *home*.

Helen's family resented James's loyalty to his extended family back *home*. Her father, a postmaster in Toronto, didn't approve of his sending for relatives—and often voiced his conviction that the Irish wanted to "take over." His opinion reflected the popular sentiment of the time. Even with their obvious advantages as white-skinned English speakers, the Irish newcomers faced opposition.

Unexpected waves of thousands of starved refugees of the Great Hunger arrived regularly, traumatized by what they had lived through. By 1850 the Irish made up a sizeable percentage of the US foreign-born population, with their presence felt most strongly in cities. These immigrants were cited as prone to alcoholism, unemployment, domestic violence, and juvenile gangs. My grandmother made sure my brother and I knew about the "Irish need not apply" signs her grandparents' generation had faced when they looked for employment. (She spoke in a tone as indignant as if these were as recent as the Jim Crow laws.)

In spite of adversity, over the following decades the Irish developed strategies for assimilation and gradually integrated into society. Acculturation is a long, fluid process that must run its course; however, markers signify watershed moments in the flow of history.

A turning point for Irish acceptability came with the Civil War—the second shard of my grandmother's memory. No wonder she had attempted to impress upon us its significance. Over 140,000 Irish-born men enlisted in the Union Army, including several of James's relatives. All-Irish units (and high numbers of Irish in other regiments) gave the clear message that Irish immigrants had cast their lot with Americans. By the time of my mother's generation, the "Irish need not apply" signs were a fading memory. And it would not matter to her parents that she married a man who was more Italian than Irish.

✦ ✦ ✦

In my mother's kitchen I wondered at the complexity of it all. A tragic famine compounded by political oppression and economic injustice. Evictions that led to the loss of homes and to leaving the land my ancestors loved. Yet here we were, blessed to recount the past. Sitting at a table in a kitchen filled with abundance, talking about a granite cross near the children's Catholic school. The family lives on.

My mother pulled out the postcards her cousins sent from their trip to County Mayo. Photos show a coastline with rocky islands, sandy beaches, and rugged cliffs. Windswept terrain gives rise to one of Ireland's holy mountains. The cousins located the ancestral home of James's parents, James and Brigid. They wrote, they even visited "*our* priests' graveyard," where James's brother and uncles and many forebears are buried.

Now, when I drive past the Celtic cross, I gather in my heart those two shards of my grandmother's memory. I honor them as evidence of the sacrifices that made our future possible. I give thanks for her insistence in passing on these threads that tie me, however tenuously and incompletely, to a past shared with the living and the dead. I hear the sound of her voice, and I picture the face of my mother. I hold onto those strands with which my grandmother held me and that she had so dearly wanted to impress upon me . . . and I make them my own.

# PART II

*It is no use saying we were born two thousand years too late to make room for Christ. Nor will those who live at the end of the world have been born too late. Christ is always with us, always asking for room in our hearts.*

—Dorothy Day

Street mural by youth from a Mexican migrant-sending town.

## Chapter Four

# Of Meals and Journeys

"How greatly I have desired to eat this meal with you" (Lk 22:15). These words echoed in my mind as my husband and I sat in the trailer of a newly arrived immigrant family. Our children played with their little girls while we discussed with them how to celebrate Rosa's *quinceañera* ("sweet fifteen" party). Navigating the nuances of spoken language and unspoken signals, I was reminded that fluency does not, alas, ensure cultural sensitivity. At the risk of overstepping our bounds, we laid out an offer: would they let us arrange a mass, and then take them out to a restaurant?

It was the mid-1990s, and emigrants from rural Mexico and Central America were arriving at destinations that had not previously experienced Latin American immigration. Our area was just beginning to integrate Spanish into its social services. My husband and I threw ourselves into the work of accompaniment. With turnover so high as families migrated in search of work, building trust meant engaging in a delicate dance of relationship whose movements must be gone through again and again.

In getting to know the family, Rosa was the one who most touched me. Since she stayed home to care for her nieces, she and I spent the most time together on my visits. When a friend donated a shell-pink, floor-length satin gown and other friends sent a check "for all your good works," I began to dream of giving her a bash to mark the birthday that many Latin American cultures define as a girl's crossing the threshold to adulthood.

Rosa knew suffering from an early age. Born the third of seven children, she and her sister shared a single pair of shoes for school, trading them off between the morning and afternoon sessions. Her father, an alcoholic, worked infrequently, and their mother left him when she tired of the domestic violence in their home. She packed up the children and walked for several hours to the nearest urban area, where Rosa's eldest brother lived with his wife and family. Rosa begged to be allowed to bring her prized possession, a pair of roller skates.

But, while life in the city was more exciting, it also proved more expensive. Unlike the village (where income could be supplemented by growing food or bartering), the city required cash. At eleven years of age Rosa left school to work in one of the factories that have replaced agriculture in their state. Even this job, however, did not provide a decent living. Her brother—hearing stories about abundant opportunity in the United States—decided to make the dangerous trip north. He offered to bring Rosa along. This time the roller skates were left behind.

After a traumatic border crossing, the family made their way to New York. Rosa's brother took a job at a dairy farm, and his wife found work at a greenhouse. Without a state-issued driver's license, he drove with one from his home country in his pocket, saying a prayer each time he set out in the car. The stress of living as undocumented workers kept them in a constant state of anxiety.

It has always struck me that the two jobs most essential to any country's ongoing survival—raising children and growing food—are the least valued. While globalization has unsettled local economies all over the world, goods and capital move more freely across borders than the people displaced by its policies.

Caring full time for her nieces, Rosa often despaired of her situation. Since their area lacked public transportation, she felt stuck. Summer had ended, but her brother resisted her desire to attend school (and wouldn't hear our explanation of services that might ease the transition). His wife's schedule took her to work before school started, and kept her there long afterward. Who would put their girls on the bus in the morning? Who would receive them after they were dropped off? Besides, he complained, hadn't Rosa already quit school back home? The tension in their home became palpable. Rosa threatened to leave.

When Jesus speaks of his desire to share a meal with his followers, each of the previous meals in Saint Luke's gospel is recalled. Some are domestic meals, like the one held in the household of the memorable arbiter of hospitality, the disciple Martha. Others are more formal affairs (Lk 9:10–17; 10: 38–42; 19:1–10; 5:27–39; 7:36–50; 11:37–54; 14:1–35). The culmination of Jesus' ministry, the last supper, is both a hospitality meal and a formal banquet, recalling all that has been learned. Each meal has led up to this moment. The cup of Gethsemane—that ultimate symbol of self-emptying—is prefigured, as are two post-resurrection meals with the gathered community (Lk 24:13–35–43).[1]

I, too, had gone through a self-emptying that year. Leaving a job I loved to devote more time to our children, my emptiness gave me the freedom to take Rosa's nieces to their first day of school and to the library or the park. It made me available to respond when Rosa called. I learned to listen—just listen—when she cried and to wait before trying out the joke that would make her smile through her tears. I tried not to confuse my dreams for her with her own perceptions of her limited choices. And I remembered that as much as I loved Rosa, her first loyalty was to her family. When her brother declined our offer but invited us to a small party at the trailer, I felt joy, not regret.

At the time I realized that this meal was not just a birthday party. It was a compendium of my life in migrant ministry. Like Saint Luke's Gospel of ten meals, where each leads to the next, we have devoured tamales made for special occasions and indulged in more cakes than (thinking of my waistline) I care to remember. This journey has led us to tables in trailer camps in the North and to outdoor kitchens in remote, dusty villages in the South.

On both sides of the border we have been fed by an extended web of friends. Inviting them to a feast, we suddenly find we have

---

[1] See Eugene LaVerdiere, *Dining in the Kingdom of God* (Chicago: Liturgy Training Publications, 1994), and idem, *The Breaking of the Bread* (Chicago: Liturgy Training Publications, 1998).

become the guests. Repaying a debt of hospitality we incurred while living in Mexico, we find our generosity being repaid in return. We are all returning the graciousness of the One who made the sun, wind, rain, and earth, and who continues to feed us with Christ's Body—a life given over fully.

Rosa looked heavenly, a feast for the eyes in the satin dress. Her family decorated the trailer with balloons and prepared a delicious meal of *mole* with rice and a tall stack of handmade tortillas. Her brother's softened manner indicated that a reconciliation had taken place. He listened to our proposal to set up the bilingual services that would help her in high school.

✦ ✦ ✦

A month from the day of the party Rosa was gone. On his way to work her brother was apprehended for driving without a license. Rosa's sister-in-law received his somber phone call. She panicked. She was overwhelmed by practical details, like picking up his car and calling his workplace. Meanwhile, her husband was turned over to immigration officials. The bail set was too high for the family to post. After being detained for a couple of weeks, he was deported.

Not surprisingly, Rosa's sister-in-law decided to go back home. Plans for Rosa to enter school were no longer needed. The money they had saved went toward plane tickets. Rosa told me not to worry. Now it was *she* who comforted *me,* assuring me that they would be all right. She would go back to school, she promised. She was determined to study, even if she has to attend night classes after working days in the factory.

Saint Luke's Gospel, a story of meals and journeys, holds the exclamation, "Blessed is anyone who will eat bread in the kingdom of God" (14:15). All the other meals we have shared have led up to this moment. All meals together afterward will bear the leftover aroma of this one. We helped the family get plane tickets; my husband drove them to the airport. A sword pierced my heart. Rosa is gone, but she left having come of age. A boundary has been crossed; bread has been broken. Blessed indeed.

# Chapter Five

# An Advent Lullaby

December afternoons grow shorter. Each day dips more deeply into darkness as we turn toward the solstice. Advent glows within the shell of winter, the most luminous time of the year. For us, as a family with young children, the allure of the approaching Christmas holidays proves irresistible.

What parent is not moved by the story of a first child's long-awaited birth? And what child is not charmed by angels and a magical star, barn animals, and kings on camels? Delighting in the season, each year we try not to succumb to its materialism. At every turn we are met with an overabundance of plastic Santas. It is easy to absorb the glib optimism of a holiday steeped in a dizzying array of consumer choices.

But the birth of Jesus in the Gospels is not the innocuous episode we make it out to be. Saint Mark's Gospel opens not with infancy narratives but with a prophet's voice crying out in the desert. Saint John's begins with a hymn exalting the time-less Logos. Saint Matthew's brief birth account almost goes un-noticed—overshadowed by the massacre of the Innocents. And, while Saint Luke's Gospel provides the setting and much of the imagery we associate with the nativity, we often overlook how this birth account (2:1–7) encapsulates the poverty, rejection, and death to be experienced by Jesus. It's like looking at a picture of the Gospel in miniature.

Through study I began to grasp how these concise verses packed with significance describe a child's birth.[1] I came to a better understanding of their meaning through a migrant family's loss.

Of the many families I have met while accompanying immigrants, I found the story of Susana and Pedro especially compelling. When I met them, the couple weighed heavy on my mind. In search of work, Susana and Pedro had left their home in a black community of Central America's Atlantic Coast. Bilingual in Spanish and English, their ethnic group is renowned for music.

While rich in culture and history, however, their home is materially poor. Pedro traveled throughout Central America as a farm laborer, making his way north. Later, the rising cost of living in their home country convinced Susana to leave their young son with relatives and join her husband.

The couple worked in Michigan, harvesting tomatoes, and then in Florida, picking citrus fruits. They were overjoyed to realize—on Susana's twenty-first birthday—that she was pregnant. But while in Georgia for the peach season, Susana told me, she experienced abdominal pain, which she knew was not normal. She made her way to a doctor. An ultrasound revealed a wonderful discovery—she was carrying twins! Their joy turned quickly to pain; the babies had not developed properly, she explained through tears. By the time they came to New York, Susana was several months pregnant but dreaded giving birth.

During the time remaining, Susana agonized over how to make sense of what was happening. They would never know for certain the reason for their children's condition. A twin pregnancy is considered high risk. Furthermore, Pedro, who was older than Susana, had been working with pesticides since his youth, a possible cause, but exposure over his years in Central America would be impossible to trace. Susana wrestled with her own hope that the prognosis would be mistaken, but as further test results came back, she began to accept its probability. She also worried about

---

[1] See Eugene LaVerdiere, *Luke* (Collegeville, MN: Liturgical Press, 1990); and Luke Timothy Johnson, *The Gospel of Luke,* Sacra Pagina series (Collegeville, MN: Liturgical Press, 2006).

how her husband would receive their newborns. An introverted man, he showed emotion through a love of music; lately, he had stopped singing.

One unseasonably warm afternoon, Susana and Pedro's twins were buried. We met at the cemetery. A handful of us huddled in silence around two tiny white caskets that resembled styrofoam boxes more than coffins. I remember thinking that the whole world should stop to mourn. Instead, the picking season had ended, and the couple had to leave hurriedly that weekend with the rest of the crew. Anonymous crosses of wood stood as the graves' only markers.

As Christmas drew closer, I found myself returning again and again in my mind to that scene in the graveyard. I could not help but compare it to Christ's nativity in the Gospel of Saint Luke. The evangelist captures the bleakness of Jesus' passion and death— while at the same time, drawing with one stroke the incarnation melded into the Eucharist. He opens the Gospel with news given in the language of his own time, that the emperor of the known world has sent out a decree. The undocumented people must be counted—so they can be taxed. Joseph and Mary must travel as migrants.

A descendant of David, Joseph arrives in Bethlehem (literally, "house of bread") with his wife, who is pregnant with the next generation of the royal lineage. But once the journey is complete, the couple is denied hospitality in Joseph's ancestral home! There is no room for the heirs of David in the City of David. There is no meal for them in the House of Bread. Returning to Joseph's native land, they are treated as strangers. Instead of coming home, they find themselves homeless. The allusion to the City of David is repeated in Luke 2:11, again foreshadowing the Messiah's rejection in Jerusalem. But salvation, too, is already being anticipated. In the shell of the most powerful empire in the world, redemption comes in the most humble of events: a child born to the poor.

Saint Luke's birth account finds a visual counterpart in Fritz Eichenberg's *The Long Loneliness*. The picture reminds me of medieval art, which often portrays several events from the life of Christ simultaneously. An angel whispers delicately into Mary's

Fritz Eichenberg, "The Long Loneliness," 1952, wood engraving, 14 ⅛" x 11½", ©
The Fritz Eichenberg Trust/Licensed by VAGA, New York, NY.

ear while her rounded belly and pained face indicate that birth pangs are already upon her. Behind her laboring figure a shining path (the *hodos,* "road," of the Gospels) snakes its way to the cross. The resurrection appears as a promise of light in the horizon. As in Saint Luke's Gospel, Mary—Mary of the mysterious annunciation, of the auspicious visitation, of the glorious Magnificat and of the prophetic finding in the Temple—appears in the foreground.

Sharing in his poverty and precarious life, she has traveled this road, pregnant with Christ. At the journey's end she arrives with her husband at the *kataluma* ("lodging"), the site of the last supper. Rejected by the City of David, Mary nevertheless brings forth her son, God's Firstborn (Col 1:15). She wraps him in swaddling clothes, as any mother would do (Wis 7:6). In a culture that practiced what we now call "the family bed," she lays him, instead, in a manger—in those days, a feeding trough hewn from stone. Even though she and Joseph are denied the traditional meal of hospitality, she offers Christ as nourishment for the flock. One can almost hear the words, "This is my body. This is my blood."

Mary has not yet been told that a sword will pierce her soul (Lk 2:35). But early listeners and modern readers alike are moved by the poignancy of her gesture, because we already know what she does not. Toward the end of this same Gospel, another journey to the City of David will reach its climax at the *kataluma* of the last supper. Just outside Jerusalem's walls, not a birth but a death will take place. Mary's loving actions will be recalled: the body of the Firstborn will be brought down from a cross. The corpse will be swaddled in linen and laid in a tomb, a cave of hollowed rock sealed with stone (Lk 25:53).

Like Susana, we already know what awaits these children born to migrant parents in the shadow of the richest empire of the world. Like Pedro, we are invited, nevertheless, to hold human fragility. As he cradled the newborns in his arms, he crooned a lullaby, singing them home.

We heard the following season that Susana and Pedro had managed to send for their son, settling year round in Georgia with relatives. As for me, I found myself one step further along that *hodos* that makes its shining way to the cross.

I think of Susana and Pedro as we try to celebrate Christmas in resonance with the entirety of the gospel message. Rejoicing at the Savior's birth, at the same time we anticipate the journey to Jerusalem, accepting the poverty and precariousness that come with it. We take in the bittersweet story of Christ's birth that the Gospel of Saint Luke so artfully conveys.

✦ ✦ ✦

As a parent, caring for my children consumes every waking moment of my days . . . .I wish I could protect other families' children, as well. And while my husband and I provide materially for our children, we also worry about their spiritual growth. My deepest wish is that our children may someday say—through the witness of their lives—"This is my body. This is my blood." While with all my heart I wish I could shield my children from its costs along the way, I point them toward the road of discipleship, where they will have their own encounters with Christ, face to face.

# Chapter Six

# Socks for Juan

In the photo he looked like any other young day laborer sitting for a snapshot to send home: baseball cap drawn over bright eyes, sneakers topped by blue jeans, a white button-up shirt accentuating sun-darkened hands and face.

But Juan—John Doe—was unlike most other migrants, and my eyes are not as observant as others that would scrutinize this same photograph during the following weeks. One friend immediately noticed that one sleeve appears thinner than the other. Juan had just died the previous afternoon, and my husband had come to help make the necessary arrangements. As instructed by the morgue, he asked for articles of Juan's clothes.

In Saint Mark's Gospel, too, clothing plays an important role.[1] Through its symbolism Jesus' disciples entered more deeply into the pascal mystery. This same symbolism became important to us in accompanying Juan's family. That night at the memorial mass the photograph came into my husband's keeping.

Juan and his brother came from an isolated indigenous settlement in Latin America where people still speak a native language. At twenty-one years of age, Juan took the exodus trail north. Crossing several borders, he wound up in Texas, where he worked as a day laborer. After six months he had saved enough to send for his nineteen-year-old brother. The two young men kept to

---

[1] See John R. Donahue and Daniel J. Harrington, *Gospel of Mark,* Sacra Pagina series (Collegeville, MN: Liturgical Press, 2002).

themselves, but when construction slowed in Texas, they decided to travel with acquaintances in search of work.

A caravan of a pickup truck and a van made their way to our area. The small crew rented a trailer in a rural area along a ravine. Not speaking fluent Spanish, the brothers had difficulty communicating with the other migrants. Their friends did not know the number of their home village's single telephone or even the name of the municipality from which they had come.

Riding a bicycle from their trailer along the winding country road, Juan was almost struck by a speeding driver. The car swerved at the last moment, but for Juan, it was already too late. Having only one strong arm, he lost control of the handlebars. The bicycle hurtled down the ravine. His brother heard the screech of brakes but did not glimpse the car, whose driver continued on. Juan's fall provoked a fatal head injury.

An inevitable question kept coming up: how could such a terrible thing have happened? Maybe it is human nature to grasp at explanations, to look for someone to blame. Because the driver did not stop. Because by the time his brother found help, the fall had already done its damage. Because Juan's arm, shriveled since childhood, failed to save him. Because malnutrition causes birth defects. Because indigenous communities like theirs tend to be poor. Because with globalization, the dollars earned in one week in *el Norte* can buy what a year's worth of corn crops cannot.

My husband explained to Juan's brother that his family had three choices: they could have Juan buried here; they could have his ashes sent home; or they could ask us to ship the body home. In stuttering Spanish, Juan's brother said that the elders of the village had to be consulted. An all-night meeting was held to make the decision. In the morning the elders told Juan's brother that the body should be sent home.

The next couple of weeks felt like a crash course. Unbeknown to us until then, immigrant communities in the United States have set systems in place to ship their compatriots who have died in exile back to their countries of origin. A whole bureaucracy is set up. The case required extensive paperwork, even though Juan had crossed the border without papers in the first place. Numerous phone calls had to be made: to his country's consulate, to the charitable institution of his home state, to two funeral homes (here *and* there). Friends in the Latino community where we lived scrambled to help my husband figure out the details.

On a local priest's referral a funeral home agreed to take the case for a lowered fee. An unseen complication arose. All connecting flights through Mexico City were booked because Pope John Paul II was going there to canonize Blessed Juan Diego. The other Indian Juan would have to wait.

Finally, all that was needed was money and contact information for a funeral home that would receive the body. My husband sat with Juan's brother in the trailer, explaining that he needed to get the name and phone number of the funeral home nearest to their village. The young man stared blankly, uncomprehending. My husband repeated the instructions more slowly. One of the other migrants finally burst in, "He doesn't know what a funeral home is." Their area was so poor that he had neither seen nor heard of one. Patiently, the friend explained to him that rich people don't wake and bury their dead at home. Funeral parlors are places where rich people go when they die.

In order to prepare the body, my husband helped his brother sort through Juan's belongings, which fit into a backpack. They found the white-sleeved shirt of the photograph and the pair of jeans, but strangely, no socks. Put simply, Juan was too poor to own a pair of socks.

The evangelist Saint Mark would appreciate the significance of this missing clothing. His Gospel uses articles of apparel to dramatic effect. John the Baptist's outfit announces that he is the new Elijah (1:6), and the beggar who throws off his cloak shows a willingness to begin a new life (10:50). The woman with the flow of blood touches the fringes of Jesus' garment in order to be cured (5:27–30). At the transfiguration Jesus' robes gleam "a dazzling white, such as no one on earth could bleach them" (9:3).

The most enigmatic mention of clothing comes with the mysterious *neaniskos*, the young man in the Garden of Gethsemane. This unnamed person has been following Jesus, wearing a linen cloth (14:51). The soldiers seize him, as Jesus has been seized. They are about to take him into Jesus' passion. But he resists, afraid to follow the Messiah into death. He abandons into his pursuers' hands the white cloth, which probably represents the baptismal garment (14:52).

Scholars have long regarded this young man as the evangelist Mark leaving his signature on the text. More recently, others see him as a symbol of the entire Christian community. True to Saint Mark's intent to call us to discipleship . . . could it be that the *neaniskos* stands for all of us? Who of us has not failed in our commitment? In scripture a member of Jesus' own circle had betrayed him, and except for the band of faithful women, most of his disciples deserted him at the critical hour.

In history, it is quite probable that Mark's community(ies), too, had at times abandoned Christ. The early persecutions shook their faith. Facing martyrdom, believers were tempted to apostasy or to name fellow Christians rather than be put to death.

In the text even the faithful women misunderstood the fullness of the paschal mystery. They come to the tomb carrying spices, even though, having been present through the entirety of his ministry (15:41), they should have seen that Jesus' body had already been prepared for burial (14:3–9). They expect to find a corpse, even though—having journeyed with him the whole way—they should have heard Jesus announce that the Christ would rise again on the third day (8:31–33; 9:30–32; 10:33–34).

Don't we, too, remain in the tomb, when we should be seeking the Living One? Seeking him together—all of us. Two thousand years ago, Saint Mark's community(ies) had to be willing to take on Christ's passion, death, and burial. Their final and most daunting challenge, however, was not to give up hope in the resurrection. This promise is symbolized in Saint Mark's Gospel by the shimmering baptismal garment . . . white as the shirt that Juan wears in his picture.

On the night of the memorial mass, Juan's brother—dressed in his best clothes (jeans, cowboy boots, and button-up shirt)—looked glassy eyed and numb. Their friends had decorated the altar with freshly picked wildflowers, candles, a bible, a large picture of Our Lady of Guadalupe, incense, and . . . the photograph. They escorted Juan's brother to the first pew, and I noticed how they treated him with solicitous compassion. During the mass the priest remembered all those who have died far from home. His homily reminded us that the scriptures write of death as a dream from which we will awake to greet Christ, a homecoming in which we won't need to knock on the door, a seed fallen into the soil that has finally come into full flower.

Within two weeks flyers bearing Juan's photograph—his immaculate shirt gleaming—were posted in Latino stores and restaurants throughout the area. I was astounded by the speed and efficiency of the campaign, carried out completely by word of mouth.

Friends fanned out to factories and farms, soccer fields, and basketball courts. An evangelical storefront church took up a collection. Miraculously, the entire, exact amount was raised within two weeks. Organizers brought back hundreds of single dollar bills and meticulously kept lists of donors. Unlike Juan, they belonged to more settled communities, immigrants helping a migrant. I kept a running tally from the ripped notebook pages with contributors' names or initials and reports from this informal web of organizers. More than five hundred people made donations, from one to one hundred dollars. The hardest-working and lowest-paid segment of the workforce, most of them earn minimum wage: the poor making a preferential option for the poor.

Juan had not been in the area long enough to be personally known to the people who contributed, but they gave, anyway. From the slenderest of details they easily grasped the precarious situation from which Juan and his brother came. They understood more quickly than I had that missing socks are clear evidence not of Juan's personal poverty, since even a day laborer would soon be able to buy a pair of socks. The missing articles of clothing represent, instead, a collective poverty. The detail that he came from an indigenous village alerted other immigrants to his family's extreme need. The fact that he was newly arrived awakened their sympathy. Over and over donors saw themselves in this "stranger."

The conversations exposed a number of issues; for example, why do immigrants have to become day laborers instead of being hired as regular employees? Another undercurrent ran through the commentaries in the Latino communities that took up the collection. Because he was indigenous, Juan faced a whole other layer of racism. One white-skinned, educated friend from Mexico explained: "You know the way *you* see *us* when we come up here to work? That's the way *we* see *them.*"

Juan's story intertwines with Saint Mark's Gospel, which tells of Jesus, the quintessential migrant. God came to earth so that we could enter heaven. The price he pays for this crossing is his own life. When Jesus is taken into his passion, the soldiers dress him in a purple cloak and crown him with thorns (15:17). They strip him at the site of the crucifixion, "casting lots" for his clothing (15:24).

After Jesus' death a follower who believed in secret made a courageous act. Approaching the very authorities who had put Jesus to death, Joseph of Arimathea won their permission and then "bought a linen cloth and, taking down the body, wrapped it in the linen cloth, and laid it in a tomb" (15:46). The rich and privileged follower finally takes a stand, placing himself on the side of the poor and powerless. The clothing of the *neaniskos* reappears, representing this time both a shroud and a baptismal garment.

When asked if he wanted to accompany Juan's body home, his brother replied that he could not; Juan's death has tied him to the migrant trail, since now he is the sole wage earner for the family.

Millions of immigrant laborers are a vulnerable (and necessary) part of our work force. Juan's family—like so many others—depends on remittances sent home by emigrants. At the same time, our own economy cannot function without them. Not only undocumented workers themselves but their employers—especially owners of small businesses—would also benefit from their regularization. So many towns and cities depend on new Americans for their vitality. Individually, immigration cases are resolved, one by one. But redemption, when it comes, will be communal.

✦ ✦ ✦

Who is guilty? Owners of small family businesses who—in order to stay afloat—hire foreign-born workers? Consumers who prefer low prices for services and produce? Immigration policies that contradict the demand for cheap labor? The corruption and poverty that dislodge citizens in developing countries from their homes? I no longer hasten to assign blame.

Juan's story is one of many stories of John Doe's who elicit an outpouring of generosity in the face of tragedy. It is not my husband's socks now buried with Juan in his village cemetery, that matter, but rather the works of mercy that went with them. And it is not only the dollar bills of the collection that add up, but the solidarity of shared grief that went into their gathering. The community will be re-vested in its baptismal garment.

When the women visit the tomb on the third day, they find a young man dressed in a white robe sitting on the right side (Mk 16:5). It is this *neaniskos* who will announce the good news of the resurrection.

# Chapter Seven

# Epiphanies
# in a Trailer Park

Would we make it in time? My husband and I packed up for a
road trip. A cooler held snacks; the car stereo, our favorite album.
Stuffing gift-wrapped presents in the trunk of a rented car, we
buckled our children into the back seat. We were off to spend the
Christmas holidays with our godchildren and their parents (our
*compadres*) in Florida. But something more than the desire to pay
a visit prompted us to drive a thousand miles. Although we could
not have explained why, we had to go. We needed to make this trip.

The snow melted as we headed south. Miles of bridges took us
through Virginia. An orange moon rose over rows of pine trees in
the Carolinas. I barely remember Georgia. Arriving at the Florida
border, we knew we would not make it. Our godchildren's family
celebrates Jesus' birth on La Noche Buena, Christmas Eve, but we
still had half the state to go. Taking a hotel room, we settled in for
the night.

Somehow I had always viewed the Magi, too, as showing up
late. In other countries the Three Kings—not Santa Claus—bring
gifts. But in the United States, Epiphany comes as an anticlimactic
footnote to the main festivities. In many households, Christmas trees
are already packed away for next year before the Wise Men even
make their way to the manger! Instead of celebrating a full season
of twelve days, we barely notice this feast which holds enormous
significance for the universal church.

The Magi seem a little lost as they arrive in Jerusalem, asking for the king of the Jews. In a real sense they are newcomers; they are only now finding their way to the faith that is a light to the nations. Though recently arrived, the Wise Men play an integral role in Matthew's Gospel. Their story opens the kingdom of heaven to the Gentiles (2:1–12).[1]

Once our children fell asleep, I snuck into the lobby to stake out the nearest Christmas tree. At daybreak, I stashed their presents under the garishly decorated artificial tree.

Christmas in Florida seemed all out of place. There was no snow on which to scatter "reindeer food" (oats mixed with glitter). Served in styrofoam cups, our traditional mug of hot chocolate tasted all wrong in the warming sunshine. Nevertheless, the children were excited to find their gifts. Tearing open the packages, they littered the floor with wrapping paper and soon demolished the stack of presents. When our four-year-old demanded, "What else is there?" my husband and I looked at each other and groaned. So much for our attempt to keep Christmas simple! Around noon, we herded the kids to the car. A long afternoon of driving took us to a dirt road leading to a migrant camp tucked amid orange groves.

Common sense directed the Magi to the seat of power, Jerusalem. After all, they were looking for a king. Little did they know that they would find salvation in the *least* powerful setting possible, a stable in a peripheral rural town.

We, too, had brought gifts—not of gold, frankincense, and myrrh, but of toys and books. Greeting the families of our godchildren, I started wondering. Who are the Magi in this scenario? The text in Saint Matthew's Gospel does not state that they are rich or royal, but in tradition the Magi are depicted as wise men and kings. The passage does not tell how many they are, either, but Christians refer to them as being three in number. Surely they must have been men of means to offer such expensive gifts. They must have come from wealthy backgrounds. Maybe they were like

---

[1] See Daniel J. Harrington, *The Gospel of Matthew*, Sacra Pagina series (Collegeville, MN: Liturgical Press, 2007).

us, leaving our home in a jade-green rental car to spend Christmas in a trailer park.

But maybe the Magi are more like our *compadres*. Maybe their journey more resembles a migrant sojourn in a dilapidated old school bus with no heat. And both our *compadres* and the Magi braved miles and miles of laborious desert. Our *compadres* come from villages whose material poverty is as foreign to us as is their cultural wealth. Years later we would visit there, making our way to remote settlements high up in the mountains. On those trips we became acquainted with the desperation that drove them from their homes. We also encountered roadside shrines, home altars, and a lovingly tended colonial-era church renovated entirely by remittances sent from the North.

As modern readers, we miss the central irony of the Epiphany story. Under the same sky, even the most learned scholars in Jerusalem did not glimpse the star the Magi had already observed long ago "at its rising" (Mt 2:2). How had pagan foreigners learned of the Messiah's coming when his own priests had not?

Saint Matthew—a Christian Jew writing for other Christian Jews—could never have imagined how his words would be used to justify anti-Semitism in subsequent centuries. Taken in their own context, they are more properly understood as directed at the seat of power in Jerusalem. For Saint Matthew, the chief priests and scribes should have been the *first* to accept the Christian revelation. Written for a Jewish audience, it gives the imperative to include non-Jewish Christians in salvation history.

As if to call our attention as well, Saint Matthew uses the word *behold* four times in the narrative. The first instance comes when the Magi arrive in Jerusalem. The chief priests and scribes knew through prophecies *where* the Messiah was to be born. The Magi knew *when*. It takes outsiders to awaken us to the present moment.

At the trailer where her family lives, our youngest goddaughter had to be cajoled to open her elaborately wrapped gift. Her brother and sister received their slender packages shyly, trying (unsuccessfully) not to break into toothy grins. The presents opened, they sat in a huddle to pore over one another's books. Their mother interrupted the reverie by sending them to retrieve their Christmas presents for our children to play with. They had gotten one gift each. Of the many things that immigrants bring to the United States, one is an appreciation of the blessings we take for granted.

The eldest, a boy, showed our son how to maneuver a remote-control car. The older girl ran reverent fingers over the cellophane packaging covering the face of her doll, dressed in crimson robes and wearing fake pearls. Our daughter marveled aloud that she had not yet taken the doll out of the box. Too happy to speak, the girl's shining eyes responded. Her silent contentment spoke volumes of joy.

The Magi, too, were "overwhelmed with joy" (Mt 2:10) when they found the child and his mother (the second "behold"). Their reaction marks a contrast: King Herod was frightened, and "all Jerusalem with him" (2:3). One can understand that Herod, known for murderous cruelty to his own family, would be jealous. And one can imagine that the chief priests and scribes—having failed to signal the Messiah's coming—might feel threatened. Saint Matthew here foreshadows the ending of his Gospel, when the Messiah is again endangered by those who refuse to read the signs of the times.

Traditionally it has been taught that this Gospel was written for communities in Diaspora. Scholars vary widely in their estimates but agree that of the millions of Jews of Jesus' time, only a fraction of them lived in Jerusalem, where a faithful remnant had remained since the Exile. All major urban centers in Asia Minor held significant Jewish populations (some, large percentages). Thousands living abroad and in outlying areas used to travel on pilgrimage to the Temple for religious feasts—as did Jesus and his followers.

But by the time of Saint Matthew's writing, the Temple was destroyed again—this time, by Rome. Soldiers had destroyed Jerusalem and pillaged the surrounding countryside. In the wake of such turmoil Christian Jews were shunned by their own religious authorities. Saint Matthew's community(ies) already lived in the Diaspora. They could no longer make the trip to their beloved Jerusalem.

At the very beginning of his Gospel, Saint Matthew recalls the fourteen generations from Abraham to David (1:17). The genealogy continues by referring to the fourteen generations from David to the deportations to Babylon. It then calculates the fourteen generations from the deportations to Christ's birth. The Messiah's arrival must be measured not only through David's golden reign but also through the destruction of Jerusalem. Reminded of this time line, listeners/readers have reason to be afraid.

In the trailer park we listen as our *compadres* retell their border-crossing stories. Our *compadre* was among the first of their village to risk the journey north. His group wandered, lost in the desert, for days. He had worked in the fields, traveling from state to state, since he was fifteen. He sent for his wife once he established himself. Shared over meals at their trailer, their accounts of hard work and tenacity opened my eyes to their reality in a whole new way. The amnesty of 1986 proved to be a blessing for this family, allowing its members to live and work with dignity, eventually becoming citizens, in the country that has become their home.

The years of travel have taken their toll, however. As parents, they have decided to stay in Florida year round, so that the children can complete the school year in one place. Relatives living in the same trailer park were obliged by necessity to keep migrating. That spring they planned to return to Georgia to pick peaches, and then try their luck in Michigan harvesting tomatoes.

From that moment on, I knew we could not go home the same way. My husband and I had to draw our children deeper into our ministry. Our pastoral approach, too, needed a change. Maybe I had unconsciously assumed that we were bringing the church to migrants when it was *they* who also freely shared the church with *us*.

Warned in a dream, the Magi go back by a different route. They do not know (as we do) that a massacre will take place, for which they are unwitting accomplices. Like the Egyptian Pharaoh who ordered the killing of Hebrew baby boys, an enraged King Herod calls for the murder of all male children in and around Bethlehem "according to the time that he had learned from the Magi" (2:16).

Joseph is warned by an angel in a dream to seek refuge in Egypt (the third "behold"), and the Messiah's family escapes a despot as cruel as the villain of the Exodus story. At the end of the narrative the Holy Family will return from exile (the fourth "behold"), echoing the Exodus story. In case listeners/readers missed the point, Saint Matthew quotes the prophet Hosea: "Out of Egypt I have called my son" (Hos 11:1) The two most salient moments of biblical salvation history come together in the person of Jesus.

The text does not give us a glimpse of the Magi's homecoming, but I suspect it was a rather mixed one. Eyes steadfastly trained on a star cannot rest on the world in the same way. Returning to their homeland, were they gripped by a sudden repugnance for its idols? Having given homage to a divine King, how could they condone the Roman Empire's ongoing wars? It would be impossible for them to explain fully to others, even those closest to them, what they had seen.

✦ ✦ ✦

I, too, have dreams: of a glove compartment full of maps and a compass pointed south. In the months that followed, my husband and I began to talk about going abroad on mission as a way to deepen our own cultural competency. We were drawn to visit the sending communities of the immigrants we met in the North. We felt—urgently—the need for a simpler setting, within a traditional culture. Most of all, we felt called to give our children an experience in a developing country. We were advised to make plans for such a change *soon*, while they were still adaptable.

Through the story of the Magi, Saint Matthew assured his community that it would never be spiritually homeless. The believers in Diaspora become the remnant. The Messiah had already crossed over and come back from the dead in a definitive crossing over. Now they must imitate their Master.

To make sense of their seemingly senseless uprooting, the remnant must look back to their stories of Exodus and Exile. But, the evangelist, reminds us, we must look, too, to our brothers and sisters in faith, the Gentiles. This Gospel ends with the risen Christ's command to go out and make disciples of "all nations" (28:19). It is time for a new crossing over.

The Magi cross over and come back, finding the Christ Child and opening the good news to outsiders. Crossing over and coming back is a remnant of Christian Jews in Diaspora, turning their gaze from their beloved Jerusalem . . . setting out to bring the good news to all nations.

For me, crossing over and coming back is two *gringos* with young children driving home from spending Christmas with their godchildren in a trailer park.

We are the Gentiles Saint Matthew had to make room for in his Gospel—written by a Jew for Jews. We are the remnant, fearful and only half willing, who must be convinced that it is time to embark on our own Exodus journeys. We are not foreigners at this ecclesial table, and we are not strangers either; together we are *compadres* in a kingdom where we are "no longer strangers and aliens, but . . . citizens with the saints and also members of the household of God" (Eph 2:19).

# PART III

*The Spirit calls me, and I must go.*

—SOJOURNER TRUTH

Dancers at a Latin American music and dance festival. Courtesy of Grupo Folklorico of Poughkeepsie.

# Chapter Eight

# A Dormitory Annunciation

Helping to prepare a young migrant for baptism, I was given a gift. Witnessing the faith of a teenage catechumen, I glimpsed an annunciation.

✣ ✣ ✣

My husband and I returned from our mission assignment in Mexico after three years. He went back to his job of providing outreach to farm workers for social services; I took to volunteering in pastoral ministry. In this capacity I met remarkable people . . . like Tomás.

Tomás came from a rural area of the Andean Mountains, where he lived with his family. There, tensions run high between an aggressive Pentecostal sect and traditional Catholicism. The result was that Tomás had never been baptized into one or the other. At fourteen years of age he left his home country in South America. Arriving in the United States, he found a job in a Southern state with a crew that tends racehorses. At first communication was difficult. Tomás, who speaks an indigenous language, had to learn more Spanish.

The crew moved from state to state, following the racing season. Tomás's applied for—and received—a special Youth Visa granted to emancipated minors. An older Latino couple whose own children were grown took him under their wing. By now, two seasons later, his Spanish had improved (he was eager to start learning English). The couple took him to church wherever the crew was stationed. Traveling to a racetrack in upstate New York every summer, Tomás began to attend mass in town.

One season Tomás confided his desire to be baptized. I met with him and the older couple where they lived in a cinderblock dormitory building with no windows. Usually painfully shy and tongue-tied in the presence of his elders, Tomás did all the talking. He expressed himself simply but with certainty.

"I want to be closer to God," he explained. "And I know that it is what God wants for me. It is my own decision."

With the support of a local pastor, a missionary priest began preparation for the sacraments of initiation. I met with the family regularly to pray with them. They inhabited one room, sharing a bathroom and kitchen with other workers. Our most contemplative moments took place when the rest of the crew had gone out to the laundromat or to the grocery store.

The dormitory was quiet, and the television was turned off. Tomás would light a candle in front of a large, beautiful picture of the Virgin of Guadalupe. We would begin by reciting the Rosary and then continue by offering spontaneous prayer. Tomás prayed in hushed tones, usually beginning in Spanish and then slipping into his native language. We ended the session by praying the Our Father in both languages.

Over the course of the prayer sessions Tomás repeated one phrase enough times for me to recognize it. Although I had no idea what the words meant, my ear learned to distinguish this particular set of sounds. It dawned on me that this was a mantra, helping to center him in prayer.

One night the dormitory was particularly quiet. The other men were out for the evening; no one was there to belittle his dialect or his awakening religiosity. The couple and I hovered silently in the background while Tomás gently uttered the familiar words. The image of the Virgin of Guadalupe stood, strong and gentle, before him. Candlelight flickered gently, casting soft illumination on his rapt face.

I asked Tomás what the phrase he so often repeated meant. He answered shyly that it would be hard to translate. It was not a formula he had learned, but rather an utterance from his heart. Roughly, it meant, "Here I am, Lord, to do your word."

Tomás had not yet had much religious instruction. He knew the basic story of Jesus' life and ministry. He was acquainted with Christ's passion, death, and resurrection. But he was still unfamiliar with the wording of biblical texts. He was unaware that he had echoed lines from the psalms and the prophet Samuel (whose mother, Hannah, sang a song of praise foreshadowing the Magnificat). And he unwittingly gave those of us who witnessed him a great gift, a contemporary reminder of the annunciation.

✦ ✦ ✦

Like a skillful painter, Saint Luke pictures Mary as a symbol of the church and of all believers. In her willingness to take on fully life's risks, joys, and sufferings—without knowing where they will lead her—we are all inspired to embrace our own vocations.

Historically, we know very little about Mary of Nazareth's life (although Christians zealously fill in missing details). We don't know her exact age at the time of the annunciation, an account poetically rendered in Saint Luke's gospel (1:26–38).[1] We can surmise that, according to custom, Mary's engagement to Joseph would have taken place by her early teenage years. Their living together would have been put off until the bride was considered old enough to bear a child.

Mary's consent to the angel's message became known as the *Fiat,* the first word in Latin from her answer, "Be it be with me according to your word," or in an alternate translation, "Be it done unto me according to your word." This acceptance of a divine invitation to participate in the Incarnation is revolutionary. The transcendent, omnipotent God being born as a human is hard enough to believe. What to make of a village woman from a conquered people voicing her acceptance?

---

[1] See Luke Timothy Johnson, *The Gospel of Luke,* Sacra Pagina series (Collegeville, MN: Liturgical Press, 2006).

The appearance of an angel in the sacred scriptures is obviously noteworthy. In the annunciation, what becomes *more* noteworthy is the way in which Saint Luke departs from the genre. Angels had appeared with important messages to other figures in the Hebrew Bible (just previously, to Zechariah in 1:5–25, announcing the birth of John the Baptist). Miraculous signs had taken place. But never had a *Fiat* been given before.

If readers remove Mary's final utterance from the story, the plot remains the same. The angel Gabriel accomplishes his task—informing the young Mary of her miraculous pregnancy. He gives her a sign in order to make this outlandish message credible. Yet the story does not end with the angel's orders. It ends with the acceptance voiced by a courageous young girl.

In a previous passage Zechariah was struck dumb for questioning the angel's words (Lk 1:18–20). Mary, on the other hand, first asks wonderingly, "How can this be?" (1:34) and then immediately agrees (1:38). Through this literary technique Saint Luke points out a novel development. His account emphasizes not only Mary's obedience, but also her agency. It is her own decision. While the trajectory of salvation history continues intact, the incarnation is unprecedented. God is doing something new.

Scholars have pointed out the possible consequences during that time for a betrothed girl who became pregnant. Readers or listeners of the early church would have understood that this *Fiat* required enormous courage and great faith. Subsequent generations have reverently meditated on the inexhaustible mystery of human and divine natures meeting in a woman's womb.

The annunciation is perhaps the most frequently depicted scene represented in Christian religious art. Capturing the imagination of centuries of artists around the world, it leads to limitless heights of contemplation. Allowed artistic license, they make the gospel scene come to life in different times and settings. Mary is often shown holding a book, although a girl of her time and background would have been illiterate. The background is often presented as a royal court, although her village surroundings were probably quite rustic.

Strictly speaking, we cannot know in a historical sense what happened. Scripturally, we have only Saint Luke's account to guide us. What was Mary doing at the moment of the annunciation? Was she shelling peas or sweeping the floor, as a girl in Nazareth would have done?

I love to view medieval scenes that show the young Mary in a richly adorned chamber with velvet drapes . . . or sitting in a landscaped garden, with an open book on her lap. Others who tend toward a more down-to-earth spirituality (like my own mother) prefer to think of her in the midst of daily life, performing household tasks. Modern scholarship gives us new insight into biblical times. Homes in Nazareth were poor; Mary's house would have been more humble than we imagine. In her village few households owned even a window (which for its covering would require precious wood, or the unthinkable luxury of glass).

I will always picture Mary at the annunciation as being in prayer, like Tomás. Pouring out her heart in the words of her people, poised in an attitude of personal attentiveness to unfolding expressions of grace. Mary's *Fiat* echoes those of her ancestors before her and inspires those of the believers yet to come. We may not be visited by angels, but all Christians are asked to give birth to the Lord in our lives. It is our decision. As Saint Luke intended, the scene prompts us to look for messages from God in our own settings. Annunciations take place all around us. Why *not* in a windowless, cinderblock dormitory?

From now on, the best image of an annunciation for me will be Tomás's face. Rapt in wonderment, deeply absorbed in prayer. Opened utterly to the Holy Spirit.

# Chapter Nine

# Family Album

If you had to pack your most important possessions into one backpack, what would you choose? I would take along my grandmother's rosary.

When I was young, my brother and I visited my grandmother each summer at her home along a riverbank in Ohio. At nine o'clock every night, before going to sleep, she would take out her rosary beads. As a child I often crawled into bed next to her. Our shapes cast shadows by night light on the walls. The smell of her house, musty in the summer heat, mixed with the comforting scent of her talcum powder. The sound of the rushing river in the backyard blended with the lull of familiar words recited in a hushed voice by a person whom I loved and trusted.

During the joys and trials of her life my grandmother remained faithful to the Rosary. Although I do not follow this practice with the same discipline as my grandmother, as an adult I have come to love the Rosary for the way it can center me in prayer. Privileged to belong to mission groups that offer accompaniment, I have witnessed the Rosary's power to console. Migrants and immigrants have taught me to value this beautiful—and formidable—instrument of prayer. With its words repeated over and over in a meditative rhythm, it can soothe the soul. Even in difficult situations it can lend peace of mind.

✦ ✦ ✦

Once my companions and I were asked by a young Honduran family to teach them to pray the Rosary. After a devastating hurricane in their country this couple had been granted temporary protected status, allowing them to emigrate to the United States. They took assembly-line jobs in light-manufacturing factories. Eventually they were able to apply for permanent residency. Settling in a small city, they began to attend our parish.

Back home, the couple explained, their particular area was wracked by violence and rife with conflicts. They had not received much religious instruction—of any kind. Besides, they had left home at a young age.

The other members of the group and I could not hide our enthusiasm at the invitation. At their apartment we practiced prayers and fingered plastic beads, thrilled to introduce these young adults to the Our Father. We read the Lord's Prayer in the Gospels, meditating on the inexhaustible depth of this prayer, beloved to all Christians. I pointed out that the Hail Mary begins with the angel Gabriel's greeting and continues with Elizabeth's exclamation. Its second half includes the title Mother of God—perhaps the oldest universal title shared by Christians to honor the Virgin Mary.

Best of all, I was able to tell the family that this tradition had begun precisely for believers like them.

In twelfth-century Europe the desire arose on the part of Christians from all walks of life to imitate the intensity of prayer undertaken in monasteries. Instead of chanting the 150 psalms, they repeated 150 prayers. Even illiterate people could join in. Over time, the format was refined and the mysteries were added. With its growing popularity the practice inspired the creation of beads from precious gems, gold, and silver. But the very first rosaries put to use were rough cords studded with knots.

That day, when we prayed the Rosary, it felt as if it were for the first time for me, as well.

✦ ✦ ✦

On another occasion, not long ago, I visited a family from Guatemala. A young brother and sister named Ramon and Sofia had asked how to apply for "Deferred Action for Childhood Arrivals." This status, which applies to undocumented young people who were brought to this country as children, offers certain protections (for example, from deportation) and privileges (such as the right to apply for a work permit). It is met by immigrant families and advocates as a welcome relief for those who live in the shadows.

Sofia had prepared a delicious soup made in the traditional style of their home state. Ramon unsuccessfully tried to keep Sofia's giggling children—his niece and nephew—from bursting in on our conversation. The good news lightened the air, and the young adults were excited to think that soon they would lead normal lives. Ramon was already saving up to buy a car when he got his driver's license.

After dinner Sofia cleared the table and led me to the couch. Then, with deliberate care, she took down from a shelf their family's prize possession: a photo album. A movie was put on for the toddlers so that we could leaf through it, uninterrupted. Ramon pulled up a chair. Sofia's hustand sat at a discrete distance. Clearly, this was an important moment.

The first pages held one large photo and two smaller ones. Their edges frayed and colors faded, the pictures were held in place by the plastic leaves of the album. Sofia paused before laying the opened book squarely on my lap.

"We carried these in our backpacks," she explained. "These were the photos we brought with us when we crossed the border."

The larger photo showed their mother, who had died soon after giving birth to Ramon. The two smaller pictures showed the grandmother who had raised them. The likeness between the women in the photos and the brother and sister in the trailer was striking. There were Ramon's eyes and chin. There was Sofia's determined expression. The likeness flitted on the faces of the children, now paying rapt attention to their movie.

The teenage brother bowed his head as his older sister recounted how their grandmother had become sick. She could no longer care for them, and the family needed money to pay for her medical treatment. Ramon and Sofia were brought by relatives to the United States. Turning the pages of the album, my eyes were met by pictures of an adolescent Ramon in a coat, hat, and gloves ("my first time seeing snow," he interjected sheepishly). I saw Sofia, dressed up for the party where she met her future husband. Together we pored over the adorable baby photos of their two children. "She has my grandmother's eyes," said Sofia fondly, pointing to a picture of her daughter. "And he has my mother's skin color," pointing to one of her son. Sofia's husband and Ramon looked on, proudly. They showed me the last, most recent pictures in the half-filled album: photos of Ramon in a cap and gown, receiving his high school diploma.

Musing over the pictures, they noted the empty pages waiting for more photos. Sofia reflected thoughtfully: "Now we can feel sure about keeping an album. We know we will be here to keep filling it up."

✦ ✦ ✦

Like a migrant family's photo album, the mysteries are treasured and precious. Sofia and Ramon carried only their most beloved pictures in their backpacks when they crossed the border. These photos remind them of where they come from and who they are. The mysteries of the Rosary remind us, even more, of where we are going.

The Latin *mysterium* is difficult to translate, and its rendering as "mystery"—connoting the concealment of truths rather than their being brought to light—does not do it justice. The mysteries of the Rosary are, in fact, more like snapshots than secrets. They are like photographs, not *hidden* but *revealed*. Although held in the intimacy of faith, they are meant to be shared.

Even though they are twenty in number, the mysteries tell a single story. Like disparate photos filling a family album, they capture significant moments in the one reign of God. The joyful mysteries recount the birth and infancy of Jesus. The luminous mysteries tell of his ministry and mission. The sorrowful mysteries relate his passion and death. The glorious mysteries orient us toward eternal life . . . and remind us that it is now up to us, Christ's followers, to continue filling the pages of the album.

Looking at the mysteries as if they were a migrant family's photo album means entering into the scenes they portray. I witness Mary's confusion and steely acceptance before the angel. I watch her embrace her cousin Elizabeth at a family reunion. I delight in the face of the newborn in the manger, and I feel immense relief at finding the adolescent, safe and sound, in the Temple. As in any family album, there is a wedding photo: Jesus appears as a guest. Another celebration places him at an even more momentous table.

Praying with the mysteries, contemporary believers enter the empty tomb with the disciples in wonder and amazement. We raise our eyes toward the Lord in a limitless sky. We wait with receptive hearts for the Spirit to descend on the gathered community.

We would much rather focus on the pleasant mysteries than the painful ones. Yet, these, too, belong in our prayer.

When they leaf through the pages of their family photos, Sofia and Ramon cannot avoid remembering the suffering and grief that also shaped their personal histories. The very first pages recall the loss of their mother at an early age and the poverty of their village, clearly apparent in the pictures. These difficult memories explain why they emigrated. They form part of their very identity. Like their grandmother's illness, which forced Ramon and Sofia to seek a better future, Christ's suffering gave us new life.

It is difficult to place ourselves in the Garden of Gethsemane or at the foot of the cross. It is unbearable to imagine the weight of rough wood . . . the choking thirst under a parching sun . . . the physical agony before a final release. I have prayed the Rosary with families who have lost a teenager to gang violence . . . or whose loved ones are being held in jail for deportation . . . or who grieve because they never got to see their dying parents one last time in their home countries. Our suffering is mystery, too, made easier to bear by prayer. Our sorrows—like our joys, our triumphs, and our insights—take their place in the human community.

Catholics believe that the Virgin Mary prays ceaselessly in heaven, joining us in the Rosary. On earth, we turn the threaded pages of a family album. The mysteries bind us in wonder. Each portrait wears the face of Love. Poring over familiar scenes, we baste our stories onto Christ's. They become part of one story, his story. The story of salvation.

✦ ✦ ✦

Every night of her life, my grandmother prayed the Rosary for me and my brother. This gesture of love on her part is one of my most treasured memories.

Cast like a lifeline over time and through space, the Rosary holds us together.

# Chapter Ten

# One Migrant's Psalm

At the time of this writing, it is the season of Lent. The passion of Jesus has come alive for me in the psalm of a young immigrant.

✦ ✦ ✦

One evening, I received a phone call. Word passed through town that a young man had been arrested. (I never cease to be amazed by the migrant community's sense of solidarity.) Several phone calls later, I found out where José was being held, and later that week, I visited him.

Making the drive to the county jail meant getting up earlier than usual. With night still darkening the windows, I dragged myself unwillingly from a warm bed. I had to keep reminding myself that I was going to visit José precisely because I *could*. Even if his relatives took time off from work to coincide with visiting hours, they wouldn't get in without proper identification. During their telephone calls they detected a growing desperation in José's voice. They feared he was becoming depressed.

During our years of advocacy my husband and I have made several prison visits, but the experience for me is never a comfortable one. As I drove for forty-five minutes on country roads, I marveled at the commitment of women and men like our priest friend who do prison ministry. I repeated begrudgingly in my mind, "I was in prison and you visited me" (Mt 25:36b), and I said a prayer for chaplains who generously perform this work of mercy.

Parking in the lot outside the building, I left my earrings and my belt in the car. Entering the front doors to the reception area, a heavy sense of confinement descended upon me. The florescent lights blared garishly. Functional-looking gray decor created a cold, impersonal feeling. The other visitors—all women and children—had already arrived. They were obviously more accustomed to the routine, and when I struggled with my locker, a young woman with long, straight hair showed me how to turn the key.

When I signed in, the guards responded civilly to my questions. They were just doing their job. They asked whom I had come to see. José's first and last names sounded strange in English on my tongue. Poor José was already losing his identity. As if reading my mind, a guard quickly rolled off José's inmate number, which he knew by heart.

I sat near two mothers, one with a school-aged daughter and another with a toddler. German shepherds on leashes prowled through the waiting area, sniffing the floor. When we were called to line up for a search, we stood within squares mapped out on the floor with tape. Visitors walked through the metal detector, one by one. When it was my turn, my metal cross set off the metal detector, and I cringed. I wear this cross when I need extra courage in ministry. But the guard who knew José's number by heart passed a wand over my torso and waved me on.

The visiting room was terribly cold. Assigned seats on stools on one side of a long bar, we were instructed to keep our hands on the counter at all times. Inmates filed in, garbed in orange jumpsuits. The school-aged girl and the toddler greeted their fathers joyfully. The young girl with long brown hair who had helped me with my locker sat next to me. Her boyfriend came over quickly. They exchanged a long, noisy kiss over the counter until a guard interrupted their embrace.

José's relatives had told him I would be coming. I made a sign to him, and we knew each other immediately.

As soon as we began conversing, I knew why I had come; I remembered how much I love this work. At first José had a hard time sustaining my gaze. His eyes looked bleary and dejected, but his gratitude was obvious. His shyness fell away. The time flew.

When I left, I, too, was overcome with gratitude—to José, for sharing so openly about his life, and to God, for giving me this chance to follow Christ in his passion more closely.

Until four years ago, when he was sixteen, José lived in Mexico with his parents and siblings on a farm. He used to travel by horse to the closest town, three hours away, where he boarded during the week in order to attend school. When this arrangement proved too difficult to maintain, going to the United States looked like an attractive option. José lived in anonymity, working and sending money home, until two months ago, when he was arrested for an infraction he claimed he did not commit.

In recent years, as immigration policies have grown more strict, even permanent residents and other documented immigrants have been deported. An immigration hold was already placed on José. This meant that once his criminal case was resolved, he would be turned over to immigration authorities. The probable outcome was that he would be forced to leave the country. In the most favorable scenario, he would be released on bail to prepare for his eventual departure. His relatives, friends, and I could only advocate for him in order to keep the case moving. Lining up legal counsel and scraping together bail money for his immigration court case were the best we could hope for. José's most urgent need was accompaniment as he faced long months of uncertainty, loneliness, and helplessness.

When I asked how he felt, José told me about a recurring dream. He dreamed he was back home in the mountains, walking behind his sister, who rode his horse. Their road came to a very steep incline—an impasse—and in the dream he found himself at the foot of a wall. José knew instinctively that there was no way around it; they had to scale solid rock. In the dream his sister miraculously made it up the stony cliff, but José, left behind, could not. (On a hunch, I asked him if he put this sister through school. He answered yes, she had just graduated.) In the dream he turned around to discover that the path behind him had disappeared. José was surrounded by stone walls, unable to move, left gazing upward, trapped in a pit.

✢ ✢ ✢

Biblical scholar Walter Brueggemann describes the psalms as songs for a journey.[1] They mirror the way that our spirituality changes—and, we hope, grows—on this sojourn.

The psalms incorporate material from before and during the time when Jewish captives were deported to Babylon. Compiled in the shadow of the Exile, they move from life in the land to slavery in a foreign country. They keep moving toward the possibility (and for some, a realization) of a return to their beloved Jerusalem.

This inner dynamism moves us, as well. As we read them, we enter not only into the adversity faced by the psalmist, who expresses individual or collective troubles, but also into the journey toward wholeness. Spiritual growth must be undergone if the crisis is to give way to renewed faith. The chaos or breakdown of life as we know it provokes a sense of disorder, but in prayer it becomes transforming *because it is addressed to God.*[2]

Brueggemann identifies three stages in the psalms: "being securely *orientated*, being painfully *disoriented*, and being surprisingly *reoriented*."[3] Psalms or portions of psalms seated in the first stage reflect normalcy and equilibrium. But the psalms would never have been written if believers remained within this stage. Sickness, war, loneliness, persecution, exile, and poverty pushed the psalmists from complacency. Those who have been comfortably settled in life only to have a crisis or an unwelcome change upset their stability can relate to this experience.

With one notable exception, all psalms follow a recognizable format. Either they speak from the reorientation stage, such as the glorious hymns of praise that sing of a mature faith in God, or they incorporate two of the three stages—with one necessarily being the disorientation stage. In a recurring pattern the psalmist begins to sing the praises of God in a comfortable narrative voice, only to give way to a tone of crisis. The new mood expresses pain, longing, fear, anger, even the all-too-human desire for revenge.

---

[1] Walter Brueggemann, *Praying the Psalms* (Winona, MN: St. Mary's Press, 1986).
[2] Ibid., 19.
[3] Ibid., 14.

Psalm 22, for example—beloved to Christians for having been voiced by Jesus on the cross—opens with painful eloquence, "My God, my God, why have you forsaken me?" Speaking from the depths of the disorientation phase, it presents almost unbearable images of grotesque suffering. However, as the psalm unfolds, it rises toward a new plateau, recalling God's mercy to previous generations. This psalm, which begins so bleakly, ends with a renewed trust in God's infinite promise of love.

The same cannot be said of the exception to the pattern: Psalm 88. Like José, who could not see a way out of his situation, Psalm 88 remains within the parameters of the second stage—mired in grim pessimism. Its stark language and use of hyperbole make very clear that the psalmist is not only imprisoned but also "stuck" (to use modern terminology, suffering chronic depression). The psalm expresses feelings of helplessness and isolation:

> I am counted among those who go down to the
>     Pit;
> I am like those who have no help . . . .
>
> I am shut in so that I cannot escape;
>     my eye grows dim through sorrow. (vv. 4,
>     8b–9a)

We know from several scripture passages that Jesus prayed the psalms; on the cross he prayed Psalms 22 and 30. In the passion narratives, once Jesus is arrested, he is led away by soldiers to await trial and sentencing. Pilgrims to the Holy Land visit a site thought to have been the high priest Caiaphas's house, where Jesus may have spent the night as a prisoner. Its ruins suggest that the subterranean floor of this house was used as a dungeon. One particularly grim discovery was a stone pit. Into this dry cistern carved from rock, unfortunate inmates were lowered by rope. The walls along the steps leading into the depths bear an inscription from Psalm 88.

Conversing with José made it easy for me to picture Jesus praying Psalm 88. Since the time of the early church Christians have imagined Jesus praying this psalm in detention, recognizing his willingness to descend into the very depths of death for us. We are reminded, also, that Christ has the power to overcome the darkness of the pit. Praying Psalm 88 as Christians, we acknowledge the reality of the feelings such as those experienced by José, pressing on our hearts with all their weight and hopelessness. Yet, we know that despair will not have the last word.

Three times the psalmist cries for help, directly addressing God:

> O Lord, God of my salvation,
> when, at night, I cry out in your presence,
> let my prayer come before you;
> incline your ear to my cry. (vv. 1–2)

> Every day I call on you, O Lord;
> I spread out my hands to you. (v. 9)

> But I, O Lord, cry out to you;
> in the morning my prayer comes before you.
> O Lord, why do you cast me off?
> Why do you hide your face from me? (vv. 13–14)

A friend who is a pioneer in Jewish-Christian dialogue and has prayed the psalms for years points out that there is one saving grace in Psalm 88: the psalmist still speaks to God. Like a drowning person who comes up to gasp for air, the verses bring us to break the surface. Rising from misery, whoever prays this psalm is, at least, still praying. And when prayer is present . . . miracles can happen.

I told José that I have seen many other immigrants go through comparable periods of imprisonment and detention. His nightmare wouldn't last forever. I tried to convince him that, at the end of his ordeal, he would be surrounded by people who care about him. I asked him the first foods his mother would prepare for him back home (at which he managed a smile). I dared to suggest that—if he allowed it to—this horrible experience would make him a better person for having gone through it. He would find new strength and maturity for his future decisions. I poured all the conviction I could muster into my words.

José listened to my advice with listless anxiety. At twenty, he had his whole life ahead of him; but to him, those months felt like an eternity.

I would never have imagined during that first visit that José would—a month later—write these words, which he gave me permission to translate and share. Reading José's letter, I recognized a familiar language:

> O Lord, at first I thought, how could this could
>> be happening to me!
> It seemed unbelievable—but once I realized it
>> was really happening,
> I knew I had to face the situation I am in.
>
> What makes me happy is the thought that I am
>> not alone.
> I keep this thought constantly in my mind and it
>> comforts me,
> and evidences of your divine love begin to arise.
>
> Thanks to the tender touch and the goodness of
>> those people who are supporting me
> and who believe in me, O God, you are already
>> helping me.
> What security I feel when I take the time to listen
>> to and to feel that soft, delicate rustling!
>
> In the quiet place of my heart, I can feel your
>> loving presence, O God.
> I don't have to carry my load alone. With every
>> breath I am filled with faith
> and I release the troubles and worries that other-
>> wise might wear me out,
> because I know that you, O Lord, are with me,
>> and I am never alone.

As an emigrant, José's life had already forced him to grow up prematurely. His jail experience led him to mature in faith. As Brueggemann writes, arriving at the third stage does not mean a return to the old order of things. It means integrating new lessons learned from the time of crisis. José attended weekly mass with fervor and prayed in his cell. He formed supportive relationships with other inmates and comforted his mother by telephone: "It grieves her to know that I am here, but I tell her not to worry." He came out of the mire of Psalm 88, ready to continue the journey.

✦ ✦ ✦

José's experience of being unjustly imprisoned, and the reality of his impending deportation, did not leave him stranded in the pit. His story is part of a much larger contemporary story—one that touches upon troubling issues of our day (signs of the times). And yet, his struggle to find meaning—to develop an authentic faith response—echoes with ancient chords. Once we become attuned to its resonance, its melody reverberates in our souls. It stirs our memory of hymns of lament and thanksgiving, reminding us of a common humanity. For Christians, the psalms remind us of our divine calling to live with Christ in eternal life. To paraphrase those lovely words of St. Augustine, quoted throughout the centuries, our hearts are restless until they reside in God.

How many of us can relate to the experience of thinking that we have it all together, only to realize that our reality has changed? We will lose our way again, and again, and, to our chagrin, find ourselves once more migrating among the three stages. Inevitably our new plateau will turn into equilibrium, and the God who "will not let us settle too easily or too long"[4] will send us on another journey. But we will not be alone. And by praying the sacred texts, our migrations—which are meaningful to us *and* to the God who accompanies us—are infused with spiritual import.

Voiced by generation upon generation, the psalms give full range to human emotions and imagination. Their lyrics remind us that God grants us moments of rest in a loving embrace but does not allow us to stagnate. We are migrants on a spiritual journey. The psalms sing us home.

---

[4] Ibid., 48.

# Chapter Eleven

# On Nightingale Mountain

For centuries, the Virgin Mary has been regarded as a star on the horizon pointing us toward the divine light. We consider her a fellow pilgrim along the path to God's reign—and our mother on the journey. If Jesus descended from heaven as the quintessential migrant, is it surprising that his mother also travels? Mary walks with us, every step of the way.

✢ ✢ ✢

> Little lamb, run to the meadow soon
> Where spring flowers already bloom.
> The flowers here do not compare
> To Mary's flowers you'll find there.

In the United States and Mexico I have attended many funerary novenas. Carried out by traditional prayer leaders, these practices are so intensely centered on Christ's passion that they echo Holy Week. The song of the little lamb reflects a softer, gentler tradition.

The song comes from a specific rural area in southern Mexico. It is sung for nine days starting on the night of a child's burial. I have heard it at novenas for children who died of cancer, accidents, crib death, and violence. Grieving parents are comforted as they absorb this terrible reality, which, for immigrant families, is compounded by migratory mourning. Its time-honored practice reassures parents that their community of faith will hold them as they take the first step of a long, arduous healing.

Accompanying any family through the loss of a child means standing near a grief that knows no words. A woman who lost a teenage son told me that even after many years the "hole" in her heart "never goes away; it just changes size and shape."

The Virgin Mary plays a consoling maternal role. Her presence assures the mourners that the "little angel" is delivered safely into loving arms. Lyrics urge the young soul to run toward the heavenly meadow. Emotions are put into words as the extended family sings:

> Her poor mother suffers affliction.
> Her father's grief has no alleviation.
> Receive her, Mother. We send home
> an angel in white, with an orange blossom crown.

Lyrics tell of flowers damp with morning dew . . . a child's swing in a laurel tree . . . a tiny fish, swimming in a fountain. They promise that the little soul—dressed in petals of white linen—will alight on fragrant rosebushes in a welcoming garden:

> Go to the garden and sing to Mary.
> She awaits there your sweet company.

Our Lady takes her place in the circle of love that surrounds the bereaved parents, just as she does in God's economy of salvation. She joins in the network of care that carries the family through otherwise unbearable days. Mary reminds us that Christ has saved us; there is nothing to fear. During this life, she holds us in the mantle of her prayer. At the end of our journey we will be brought fully into the presence of her Son.

✦ ✦ ✦

A song about a celestial garden eases loss; the memory of a stone cottage in an olive grove shimmers with lucidity. The mother of God awaits in both.

From earliest times Christians have recognized in Mary not only the mother of a human being named Jesus, but the mother of God. Mary's most ancient title, *Theotokos,* literally means "she who gave birth to God."

For centuries, believers have wanted to know more about the life of the Virgin Mary. Questions were enkindled in the Christian imagination. Where did she go after the Crucifixion? How did she spend the rest of her time on earth? Saint John's Gospel simply states that Christ gave Mary to the beloved disciple, "and from that hour the disciple took her into his own home" (19:27).

While unsubstantiated historically, an ancient tradition illumines Mary's life after Pentecost. Scholars cannot verify this claim, but many Christians believe she spent her final days at a site outside of Ephesus known as the House on Nightingale Mountain.

Some eighteen centuries after the time of Saint John's writing, an invalid nun from Germany, a woman who had never traveled abroad, had a vision. Speaking a language later identified as Aramaic, Sister Anne Caterine Emmerich described a stone house where, she said, Mary spent her final years. Emmerich's vivid accounts sparked interest, and in the late nineteenth century an expedition went to Turkey. There, in an olive grove outside Ephesus, they found the ruins of a stone cottage on Nightingale Mountain.

Saint Luke's verse that Mary "treasured all these things in her heart" (2:51) paints the image of a contemplative woman. Devoted to constant prayer, she was present when the Holy Spirit descended on the community (Acts 1:14). Mary was centered in intimate communion with Christ—who himself prayed in an olive grove. Catholics (and others) believe that at the end of her life, this communion continued unbroken, delivering Mary across the border of death. Christians of the first centuries celebrated our Lady's crossing of the ultimate threshold in the assumption.[1]

---

[1] My favorite reference for history of Marian devotion is Jaroslav Pelikan, *Mary Through the Centuries* (New Haven, CT: Yale University Press, 1996).

The early church built shrines where martyrs had lived—and even more, where they died. But the mother of God could not be confined to one place. Her tomb is nowhere, and she belongs everywhere. Unlike localized holy figures, she is *our* Lady. The assumption cemented this nascent universal identity. Jesus' words from the cross were already understood to mean that God gives Mary as mother to the community of believers.

✢ ✢ ✢

At Bülbül Dag (Nigthingale Mountain), pilgrims are greeted by silvery trees that populate a hillside olive grove. A freshwater spring flows, said to have sprung up in Mary's own room. At the Petition Wall pilgrims leave scraps of paper asking for intercession from the saint who spent her life on earth in prayer and who continues to pray for us in heaven.

Because of the lack of definitive evidence, the church recognizes Nightingale Mountain simply as a holy site. There is no clear historical record that the Virgin Mary and Saint John lived in Turkey. The Jerusalem tradition, which proposes that Mary remained there until the end of her life, remains a credible one. Then, why are we willing to believe that Mary spent her last days at the House on Nightingale Mountain? Popes Leo XIII, Paul VI, John Paul II, and Benedict XVI have each made a pilgrimage here.

My intuition is that Christians find a credible image of the mother of God in this picture of Mary. We can find her listening with rapt attention to birdsong in an olive grove. A widow whose only Son is gone, she is well-acquainted with sorrow, loneliness and solitude . . . yet, these have not conquered her. Instead of numbing her capacity for contemplation, they sharpened it.

She sits, whole body alert, resting in a deep recess of peace. Its silence is pierced only by the song of nightingales. Afternoons, olive trees shimmer in the sunlight that falls gently on the side of a hill. Like others who have pictured her in this home on the outskirts of the city of Ephesus, I can easily imagine Mary in the House on Nightingale Mountain.

A friend who leads groups to Turkey points out, since traditions place her in both Jerusalem and Ephesus, that it is possible that she traveled between the two. What if, since Mary would have been in her late forties or early fifties at the time of Jesus' death and resurrection, she remained active for a couple more decades?

The scriptures give us pictures of Mary as a young girl, a radiant new mother, a worried parent, a disciple on an exhilarating and bewildering journey of faith, and a grieving witness at the foot of a cross. In doing so they describe her in the terms of her Jewish identity—a history told through stories of human mobility.

Mary's portrait in the scriptures begins with a journey, the trip to visit her cousin Elizabeth. Each of the four evangelists portrays the mother of Jesus in his own way, according to his unique christological focus. They concur in placing her on the Way. Mary joins Christ in his itinerant ministry, following him along the journey to Jerusalem. Since Mary journeyed with Jesus, it is conceivable—if unverifiable—that she joined the early Christian Jewish communities in the Diaspora. By the third quarter of the first century, it was already clear that the future of Christianity lay not in Jerusalem, but in the network of local churches outside of the Holy Land. Saint Paul and other missionaries had visited Jewish enclaves throughout Asia Minor, preaching in large and thriving Diaspora communities—including Ephesus. Christians there had a strong devotion to the Virgin Mary.

An ecumenical council in Ephesus would formalize Mary's title *Theotokos* (Mother of God). The patriarch Nestorius had been arguing that Mary was the mother of *Christ* but not of *God.* While some two hundred bishops met to clarify the matter, the people of Ephesus made their voices heard. Men, women, and children took to the streets chanting, "Holy Mary, mother of God."

Whether Jesus' mother spent her final days in Jerusalem or in Ephesus, Christians instinctively know that she belongs with us, on the Way.

The House on Nightingale Mountain tradition locates Mary within the Diaspora. She shared fully the church's experience of human mobility. To use contemporary terms, as migrant, asylum seeker, or refugee, and at the House on Nightingale Mountain, immigrant. We imagine her willingness to travel with us, her children, into exile or exodus. No matter how perilous the journey or how painful the loss, we find her at our side.

✦ ✦ ✦

I once heard the testimony of an emigrant from Ecuador (now a naturalized citizen) who told how Mary "appeared" to her in a time of need.

Twenty years ago this woman and her husband were newly married. Although they were college graduates, they came from rural settings where their families lacked the resources and the connections to launch them into careers. The young couple decided to go North.

Her parents tried to talk them out of the idea but soon realized that they could not dissuade the newlyweds. The couple made their preparations. Her father took special pains to reinforce the stitching on his daughter's backpack and the soles of her shoes. At daybreak that morning, he gave her the traditional *bendición*—blessing. Then he bent down and slipped her shoes onto her feet, saying: "The Virgin will be with you. Never forget that."

The young couple's trip took several weeks. Along the way a corrupt official allowed them to continue their journey—but not before emptying their pockets. They reach the US border in low spirits and out of money. They debated whether to call home, but how could they tell their poor parents they had not eaten in two days?

Suddenly the thought of her father's gray head, bent lovingly over her feet, came to the woman's mind. With sudden insight, she slipped off her shoes, which were worn and cracked after walking many miles. Lifting their inner soles, she found a strip of paper protected by plastic wrap onto which her father had written their telephone number in case she did not make it through the desert. She also discovered a folded bill of money and a holy card of the Virgin Mary. Her father was right. The Virgin had been with her all along.

✦ ✦ ✦

Mary, the mother of God, is our mother, as well, mother to the body of Christ. Not only in Mexico, Turkey, or Ecuador, but wherever Christians recognize in hers the face of their mother— full of tenderness and love. And just as centuries ago, when we lift our eyes to hers, the *Theotokos* makes sure that we encounter her Son as well.

# Chapter Twelve

# Welcome, Holy Family

> In the name of heaven,
> I ask of you shelter
> My beloved wife
> Can go on no longer.

Every year during Advent, these archaic-sounding lyrics are sung in Spanish in Latino communities of various denominations all around the United States. I most enjoy hearing them in farm-worker camps. The word for *inn* in Spanish is *posada*. Las Posadas, a nine-day celebration, beginning December 16 and ending December 24, symbolizes Mary and Joseph's cold and difficult journey from Nazareth to Bethlehem and their search to find shelter.

Originating in Spain, this yearly tradition is now found in many parts of Latin America. It is based on Saint Luke's birth narrative, which states, "There was no place for them in the inn" (2:7). Recited for generations in the Spanish-speaking Southwest, Las Posadas are only now being introduced to other regions in recent decades by newly arrived immigrants.[1]

---

[1] Our nation's first Catholics were Hispanic. Today, 70 percent of Latinos are neither migrants nor immigrants (see Timothy Matovina, *Latino Catholicism: Transformation in America's Largest Church* (Princeton, NJ: Princeton University Press, 2012). For documentation of one state's first Mexican influx, see, for example, Robert Courtney Smith, *Mexican New York: Transnational Lives of New Immigrants* (Berkeley and Los Angeles: University of California Press, 2005).

When a congregation of sisters suggested holding a Las Posadas celebration on the farms in our area's wine country, the response was immediate and positive. Families signed up and the news passed quickly by word of mouth. Participants form two groups, pilgrims and hosts, divided by a closed door. As a bitterly cold wind whips across the grape arbors, gloved hands clutch candles that keep getting blown out. Voices—muffled by layers of scarves—waver in freezing temperatures. From inside their home the hosts respond to the pilgrims outside,

> This is no hotel!
> Continue along the road
> I cannot open to you:
> You might be a rogue.

The exchange continues:

> Don't be inhuman.
> Have mercy! If you do,
> God in heaven
> will surely reward you.

The chorus inside rudely replies,

> Move along,
> And don't keep asking,
> Because if you do
> I'll give you a thrashing.

All over the country—as the United States absorbs new waves of immigrants from various countries—local governments, churches, social services, community organizations, employers, and law enforcement "make room" for newcomers. Once again, the United States proves itself a land of opportunity. But assimilation does not happen without friction. At one time or other, many can relate to Mary and Joseph's feeling like unwanted guests. The colorful verse invariably elicits a laugh.

As a popular custom this practice is usually led by laypeople. Most of our participants come from agricultural communities in their own places of origin. The early 1990s saw the dismantling of rural support systems in Mexico and Central America, and the Free Trade Agreement took effect in 1994. By 1995 the demographics of agricultural labor in the United States reflected a change. The aging farm-worker population was being replaced by new Latin American emigrants seeking work in *el Norte.*

Las Posadas—which has become synonymous with Christmas in Mexico—represents the inculturation of Catholicism in native spirituality. A Spanish substitution for the nine days of processions and solstice rites honoring the sun god Huitzilopochtli, it was promoted by Franciscan missionaries in order to illustrate a new, Christian content. In a contemporary analogy, the wrapping paper was recycled but not the gift inside.

Piles of snow and sheets of ice on dirt roads posed a challenge, but somehow we managed to carry out all nine nights. One night a blizzard struck, making highways impassable; families trudged through the vineyards on foot, carrying trays of food and five piñatas. Each night, more people arrived; by the end, it was standing room only in trailer living rooms or dormitory kitchens.

Las Posada statues remain in the home that receives the pilgrims until the following night, when the scene is reenacted at another place. One night's hosts become the next night's guests, with families take turns delivering and receiving the statues and the pilgrims who travel with them.

One young woman offered the use of her family's Holy Family statues, which had been carried in a backpack across the border. On the arduous journey across deserts, mountains, and a river, the statues got chipped and Saint Joseph's hand broke off. Like immigrants themselves, she summarized, the statues are "battered, but still here."

In the two-chorus song, stanzas begin to reveal the identity of the pilgrims. Many of them did not know each other before, but now they stood together against the cold. Shivering pilgrims intone:

> We are worn out
> By the trip from Nazareth.
> I am a carpenter,
> My name is Joseph.

This does not move the hosts inside one bit:

> Just let me sleep—
> I don't care about your name!
> We will not open the door.
> I won't tell you again.

The singers taking the part of Saint Joseph become more desperate:

> Dear man of the house,
> The queen of heaven tonight
> Begs of you shelter
> For just one night!

But the response from the other side of the door remains harsh and unfeeling:

> Well, if she's a queen
> Who sits on a throne,
> At night why does she
> Travel all alone?

Once when my husband was asked to name farm-worker women's most pressing health-care problem, he replied unhesitatingly, "depression." On winter nights, when the seasonal work has slowed, the dark of night descends unmercifully early, and the cold—harsher here than in a city—leads to a sense of isolation. Recently arrived immigrants of all cultures are often unprepared for the loneliness they are prone to experience during their first holidays away from home.

At first, I attributed the success of Las Posadas to the overcoming of this sense of isolation. There is an obvious joy in recreating a beloved tradition far from home, in gathering together a small but growing circle of friends, and in partaking of sweet breads and boiling hot coffee, a heated punch *(ponche)* seeped in stewed fruit, steaming hot tamales, and other traditional foods . . . upon finally entering the home once the banter of the song is completed. The warmth and light and familiar aromas provide an unmistakable sense of comfort and celebration.

But as the days went on, I began to perceive something else. The turning point in the song comes with the revelation that Mary is the mother of the Savior. Even as they voice her name, participants open new possibilities.

The pilgrims outside (by now, half frozen and eager to enter the warmth and light on the other side of the door) sing Joseph's part:

> My wife is queen of heaven
> And her name is Mary.
> Mother of the Divine Word
> She is soon to be.

Mary gave hospitality to Christ himself in her own body! Her name signals a shift taking place. With this—the mystery of the incarnation—everything changes. Hostility is suddenly and surprisingly transformed into eager hospitality. The inside chorus replies, in a burst of familiarity and largesse:

> Are you Joseph?
> Your wife, Mary, is with you?
> Enter, good pilgrims;
> I did not recognize you!

In recognizing the hidden presence of Christ borne in Mary's womb, strangers are no longer unknown but called by name. Hospitality is no longer a favor to be granted or refused, but rather a privilege that a host is able to extend. The song now confers a blessing upon the house that receives the pilgrims:

> Gentle folks, may God repay
> your generosity,
> and may heaven bless you
> for your charity.

The hosts reply that the presence of the Virgin is its own reward. Mary's special role in salvation history is lifted up as a source of blessing to all humanity, in an entirely intimate way:

> Blessed is the house
> That shelters this day
> The pure Virgin,
> The beautiful Mary.

When the pilgrims finally entered the house, we began with a short prayer. A scriptural reading in keeping with the spirit of the Advent season followed. Participants spoke of taking Christ into our hearts, and giving God a place in our lives. Intercessions and the Lord's Prayer concluded the simple service.

One year, an uncanny coincidence took place. We knew that two women on different farms came from the same village; we did not know that they were related. One came along to the celebration, which was being hosted by the other. They had not been together, or even spoken, since leaving their home country. Not only were the two women cousins, but unbeknown to each other, they were both expecting. The religious sisters prepared the biblical texts for every night. The scriptural reading happened to be the visitation (Lk 1:39–56), where a pregnant Mary visits her also pregnant cousin Elizabeth.

For many Spanish-speaking families I know, Las Posadas staves off depression as immigrants reminisce together about their respective homelands. They introduce workers from different farms to one another and give children a chance to taste the traditions (literally) of their parents' places of origin. They allow people who do not always feel welcome to be overwhelmed by hospitality. The hospitality of the rural poor is legendary, and I have vivid memories from Latin America of being pressed to occupy the only chair in a house. But there is more. Only by the last couple of nights did it dawn on me: the secret to Las Posadas lies in the joy of becoming a host.

Fifteen years ago, my husband and I mused, we could not have recruited nine families who felt settled enough on the farms to host Las Posadas for friends and strangers. In this setting, so far from their places of origin, becoming a host is a sign of victory. Like Joseph, the fathers of these families are among the few farm workers who have brought their wives with them instead of leaving them behind. Like Mary and Joseph, these parents seek a place for their children, having "settled out" of the migrant stream (Florida, Georgia, Michigan, the Carolinas) instead of following the crops. Earning the esteem of their employers and co-workers, they have made relationships that fill these trailers and dormitory kitchens with light, laughter, and love.

✢ ✢ ✢

Proposals for immigration reform often talk of "guest-worker programs," and certainly many farm workers welcome the security and advantages of sanctioned agricultural programs. But the families of the Las Posadas being sung all over the United States are not only guests. They are hosts. They are hosts who have made homes for their families in the new communities where they have already become contributing members. Advocates who insist on integrating a "path to citizenship" in immigration reform draw upon this insight. Emigrants become migrants, who become immigrants, who become residents . . . then citizens. Eleven million more people wait in hopeful expectation.

What could be more human than entering the give-and-take of guest and host? And what could restore our dignity more than the thought that we are asked to make room for God's own Son, that we—unworthy and recalcitrant and inhospitable as we are—are suitable dwelling places for the ultimate Guest?

God came down, entering humanity, in order to raise humanity up; by receiving Christ this season, the liturgical year once again gives us the awesome possibility of becoming host to the Word-made-flesh.

> Enter, holy pilgrims,
> Receive this corner, set apart.
> For though my dwelling is poor,
> I offer it with all my heart.

# PART IV

*Give me your tired, your poor*
*Your huddled masses yearning to breathe free*
*The wretched refuse of your teeming shore*
*Send these, the tempest-tost, to me*
*I lift my lamp beside the golden door!*

—EMMA LAZARUS

Mother Cabrini's carriage, used for transporting orphans.

# Chapter Thirteen

# Food for the Journey

Few things have the power to move me like watching a communion line.

Having attended many churches, I have witnessed this slow shuffle toward grace in different settings. Watching its steady progress toward the altar, I never fail to be mesmerized.

Some communicants inch forward with reverently folded hands. Others amble along with careless posture. The elderly have made their way to this sacrament for a lifetime; I envy their indomitable discipline. Others are middle aged—like me, old enough to have taken on life's burdens. I look for signs of the weight they surely carry on their shoulders. Young people vary the most in their demeanor. Some faces reflect intense piety, others, routine boredom. My favorite are very young children. When they finally arrive at the front of the line, they take a single, long stride, heads bobbing into place as they stand, hands outstretched, ready to receive.

For my first communion, forty years ago, I learned to kneel at a guardrail and extend a flattened tongue. As changes in the liturgy were implemented, the nuns in our school taught us to make a shallow basket of our hands, a "throne" of palms and fingers. Our incredulous reaction ("touch the host with our hands?") faded as we adopted the new posture with reverence. In a gesture I particularly love, my children bow before their turn, a habit they learned in their own school.

Although this has been my weekly practice for over four decades, the mass rarely becomes an expression of rote repetition for me. Even at the parish my family attended for fifteen years, no two celebrations were exactly the same. The songs led by the choir, the readings, the liturgical time of year, the weather and the "goings on" outside church doors set the mood for the liturgy. Events in my own life, too, imbue the ritual with meaning. We bring our particular, embodied lives to the altar, each of us with our own intentions.

The rubrics (fine-tuned over centuries) welcome me to a familiar rhythm. Recent changes to the translation give me pause, but the flow of the liturgy sweeps me along in its progression. Moving from moment to moment, they allow for a full emotional range. Their repertoire takes me through repentance . . . insight . . . catharsis . . . fellowship.

The high point of the liturgy arrives. The celebrant's hands extended, the Spirit comes. The transcendent *happens*. With the consecration, Jesus is—inexplicably, miraculously—among us. In his presence, we gain the courage to address the ineffable Creator of the universe as our Father. We make peace with each other, and we pray for the world. Dropping again to our knees, we acknowledge that none of us is worthy to receive the Lord—God's great giving of Self. And then, we join the communion line.

How hard it is to sustain human awareness of the divine Presence! The communion line betrays this difficulty. It is easy to witness the fervor of people who approach with obvious devotion, focused wholly on the sacrament. More often than not, however, our attitude is casual. We trip over the kneelers and brush past others in the pews. We try not to step on the heels of the person in front of us. We fumble forward. My ethereal experience of only a few moments ago melts into a meditation on the color of the church carpet.

Perhaps that is why I so love to watch. My own faith is paltry. When I allow my gaze to be distracted—as I inevitably do—I lose my grasp on the thin thread of contemplation. But the communion line is not about me. It is about God, who leaps toward us with great strides. And about God's people, whose ridiculously small baby steps along the journey please the Lord so immensely that with each move we make . . . Christ surely smiles.

Here we come, slouching toward paradise. Imagine God's un-fathomable generosity, *still* willing to come toward us! And when we arrive, we realize . . . he has been with us all along.

Christians believe that the Body and Blood of Christ are food for our earthly journey and also a foretaste of the heavenly ban-quet. Whatever our difficulties, we must rise. Stirred, sometimes unwillingly, we stand up. We leave the complacence of our pews to take tiny, slow steps toward new life. This act takes initiative, courage, and steadfastness. It does not always feel like a tran-scendent experience (even though it always, always is). I think to myself, hunger and thirst are also tedious.

Traditionally, in preparation, Christians refrain from eating or drinking before communion. The rigorous discipline of our parents' and grandparents' generations, who fasted from midnight onward, is no longer required. As I grow older, I appreciate more and more its symbolism. As the saying goes, Why bring your cup to the well if it is already full?

I look for the moment when hunger and thirst meet Christ's Body and Blood. Like a gift eagerly awaited but not guaranteed, its fleeting expression never fails to surprise me. Each time, I am transfixed.

If you watch for it carefully, you will see it—even on the face of the teenager from whom you least expect it. All of a sudden I glimpse that yearning, that fragile expectancy. A suddenly opened face as hands and mouth receive. A blossoming of trust. The pos-ture of a child or adult in complete absorption, fully present to an encounter with the God whom we love: *communion*. It takes my breath away.

✦ ✦ ✦

I have come to think of the communion line as a migration. Christ is present, but we must *seek* him. We leave our pews, will-ing to be led to wherever *he* is. And when believers find it hard to put one foot in front of the other, we can take confidence in an extraordinary consolation. *He* has already come to *us*.

And . . . Christ is about to send us. The slow migration to the altar rail will propel us along its continuing trajectory—to serve in the world.

Once my husband and I had just gotten our small children ready and dressed for church—as any parent call attest, no small feat. We were buckling them into their car seats when my husband received an emergency phone call. The caller, a victim of domestic violence, wanted out—*now.* Could my husband come pick her up? Although we would not make it to the early mass, I remembered thinking, we were already being *sent.*

Christ will take our hunger—and sharpen it. He will ignite our thirst—and leave us more parched than when we came.

We give him our longing to be filled with his presence, to be so close to him that he becomes part of our very bodies. To paraphrase Saint Paul, to no longer live in him but *he* in *us* (Gal 2:20). We turn over our personal inadequacies and our problems. Our hope of providing better lives for our families. Inevitably concerns for my children surface, and I hand them over. I admit the anxieties that gnaw at my soul, and I shake loose the spiritual stupor that numbs my mind and heart. I rise to move forward, undertaking a journey, carrying all that I own.

Shuffling toward grace in the communion line, we bring with us not the pride of possession but the meagerness of what little we have. Jesus works miracles with even the most limited of offerings. Perhaps after all is said and done, hunger and thirst are our most important gifts. In the communion line, we give them to the Lord. He will use them to feed the world.

Standing in line, I acknowledge my need to be fed. I am hungry, Lord, feed me. I thirst; give me to drink. I came not because I am satisfied, but because I want to be made full. I came to find you. Here is my brokenness, my sin, my failure. Here, also, is my desire.

Fed by boundless love, I trust that there will be enough grace to carry us through.

We go back to our seats, but even if we retrace our steps, we return home by a different route. We have joined the great march, traveling toward the day when all hunger and thirst will be sated at the Bridegroom's feast.

# Chapter Fourteen

# And You Welcomed Me

On a trip to New York City, I was stopped in my tracks by an unexpected sight. We were visiting St. Patrick's Cathedral. A guide took us behind the altar to descend into the cathedral's crypt. Of the men buried there, most were immigrants. All served immigrants. Reading Irish and French surnames on identifying plaques, one, in particular, caught my eye: Pierre Toussaint.

In moments like this one, I love the church, which places a former slave next to an archbishop. A church that celebrates holy men and women of *any* color, country, or language—for emulation by people of *all* colors, countries, and languages. A church that takes to heart the Lord's call to hospitality in the Great Judgment. The basis for the traditional works of mercy, in this text Jesus says, "I was a stranger, and you welcomed me" (Mt 25:35).

Venerable Pierre Toussaint was brought to New York from French Haiti as a slave. After gaining freedom, he and his wife provided generously for the needs of the poor—many of them, recently arrived from various countries of origin. Their piety became widely known, and numerous acquaintances sought his advice as counselor and confidant.

A successful businessman, Toussaint bought freedom for countless slaves. His charity and generosity went beyond remarkable toward the miraculous. When the family he had belonged to lost its property in Haiti, he even provided from his own means for the impoverished widow of his former master. Beloved to the local Catholic community during his lifetime, Toussaint was buried in the cemetery of the original cathedral. When the new construction was built, his remains were moved (along with the others) to rest in the new crypt.

In the development of the US church, figures like Pierre Toussaint make our history come alive as a church of immigrants. My personal favorites include two religious sisters, a priest who was my own relative, a bishop, a single mother, and a married man who fathered seven children. These few, brief stories tell of men and women who welcomed Christ in the stranger.

✦ ✦ ✦

Saint John Neumann was born in Bohemia (the modern-day Czech Republic). At the time he entered the seminary, his bishop discouraged ordinations; Bohemia had a surplus of priests. Neumann immigrated to the United States, where he was ordained in New York in 1836. He then spent four years ministering to recently arrived German settlers. The experience was formative. Neumann joined the Redemptorists, a missionary order with a charism for preaching that had been founded to serve the rural poor. He became a shepherd for immigrants.

Working as a parish priest in New York, Maryland, and Pennsylvania, Saint John encountered Catholics from all over Europe. His gift for languages was put to excellent use. Along with German and Dutch parishioners, he also ministered to Italians (having learned their language fluently in Bohemia). Neumann even studied Irish in order to hear the confessions of coal miners who did not speak English. As bishop of Philadelphia, he is credited with founding the first parochial school system and numerous parishes.

Saint John's frugality became legendary. Sharing the poverty of his flock, he wore the same pair of boots throughout his life in America. His responsibilities implied an enormous burden—one he carried with humility. Anti-immigrant fervor reached new heights during his episcopate, with nativists setting fire to convents and schools. Neumann wondered if his leadership could weather such a tempest. He wrote to Rome asking to be replaced. The Holy See trusted him to continue.

The sacrifice of his service took a toll. In 1860, at forty-eight years of age, Neumann died of a stroke while running errands on the streets of Philadelphia. He is the first American bishop and male US citizen to be canonized.[1] Saint John is often held up as a model of pastoral care for immigrants.

✦ ✦ ✦

Like Saint John Neumann, Saint Frances Cabrini is remembered for extraordinary ministry to immigrants.

Frances Cabrini was born in 1850 in northern Italy to a farming family. A premature baby, she was the tenth of eleven brothers and sisters (most of whom did not survive adolescence). From an early age Cabrini dreamed of going to China as a missionary. Her parents allowed her to attend a boarding school run by religious sisters, and she petitioned to join their order. The request was turned down because of her poor health. Cabrini studied to become a schoolteacher and was given charge of an orphanage run by the diocese. The arrangement facilitated her entry into religious life along with five other young women, who made Cabrini their novice mistress. They would become the Missionary Sisters of the Sacred Heart of Jesus.

Clergy encouraged the fledgling community to work locally, but Saint Frances had other ideas. The childhood dream of foreign mission tugged at her heart. She had taken the religious name Xavier in honor of the great Jesuit missionary Francis Xavier. Cabrini sought advice in Rome. An Italian bishop had initiated pastoral care for emigrants abroad and invited her to consider this work. The calling was confirmed when Cabrini was granted a papal audience. Pope Leo XIII told her to go, "not to the East, but to the West."

Saint Frances and her sisters arrived at New York to find that Italian immigrants lived in dire poverty. They spent their first

---

[1] While Saint John Neumann and Saint Frances Cabrini were the first US citizens to be canonized, the first *American* saint had already been declared: Rosa of Lima (1586–1617).

night in a tenement in Manhattan's infamous Lower East Side. The local church had not expected them to arrive so soon, and pastoral care for Italians was in a rudimentary stage. Furthermore, the community they served faced daunting challenges. Like other immigrants at the time, Italians took dangerous, low-paying jobs. They suffered discrimination from others who regarded them as "not quite white." The population was considered to have high rates of illiteracy (in both Italian and English), domestic violence, alcoholism, and delinquency.

Within a short time the sisters founded numerous projects. Other women's congregations and wealthy donors supported their orphanages, convents, schools, clinics, community centers, and hospitals. An anecdote about Saint Mother Cabrini reveals her resourcefulness. The Jesuits sold the congregation a piece of property at a reasonable price because it lacked a water supply. To everyone's surprise, Cabrini—the daughter of farmers—discovered an underground spring with plentiful water.

Another legend tells how the sisters began in health care. The archbishop of New York asked Mother Cabrini to consider hospital work. She held off, hesitant to take on another ministry. In a dream she saw the Virgin Mary tending to a patient in a hospital ward. Saint Frances asked what she was doing, and the Blessed Mother responded, "I am doing the work you refuse to do." Soon the Missionary Sisters became known far and wide for hospital work!

Like Saint John Neumann, Mother Cabrini became an American citizen. And like Saint John, she made room in her heart for all peoples. Her ministry extended beyond its original population. The Missionary Sisters of the Sacred Heart spread to many other parts of the United States and to several other countries, where they continue to serve.

After a long and very active life, Mother Cabrini died in Chicago in 1917 at the age of sixty-seven, while preparing Christmas candy for children. The patroness of immigrants became the first US saint.

✦ ✦ ✦

The story of my mother's great-uncle illustrates a similar pattern at the turn of the twentieth century.

Vitus entered the seminary as a teenager in his native land (Slovenia, in the former Yugoslavia). At the same time, across the Atlantic Ocean, bishops in the Midwest debated how to serve the recent wave of Slovenian immigrants. An Ohio diocese sent word of the need for clergy. Young Vitus rose to the challenge.

Vitus came by ship to the United States to finish his seminary studies and was ordained. Having come to shepherd his people, Fr. Vitus embarked on his mission with zeal. The immigrant community responded overwhelmingly. In a short time a Slovenian parish was founded, with him as its pastor. The congregation grew quickly, with English-language classes, social services, and a host of devotional societies. Welcomed in this setting, the immigrants felt a sense of security, while at the same time integrating into their new life in the United States. The still-young Fr. Vitus was named a Monsignor, and even given the honor of being addressed as "Right Reverend."

Differences arose within the parish shortly after the turn of the century. The community's exponential growth during a very short time led to "growing pains." By 1907, the parish was embroiled in arguments over finances and staffing. Parishioners had little understanding of how parishes and schools were run in the United States, as opposed to "back home." Stones were thrown (both figuratively and literally). At one point some five thousand Slovenians dressed in traditional attire (mistakenly identified as Polish in one newspaper article) marched on the Chancery.

Subsequent pastors oversaw the changing needs of the community, which continued to grow. A bilingual commemorative book printed for the parish's anniversary shows early photos of parishioners grouped in an array of activities. At its height the grammar school enrolled two thousand students. By 1930, it was the largest Slovenian parish in the country.

Meanwhile, Fr. Vitus—now in another parish—brought his brothers and sisters to America. Their children married into families of Cleveland's established Irish population. Fr. Vitus's nephew,

Martin—a voracious reader—would have followed in his uncle's footsteps if he hadn't gone blind as a teenager. (My grandfather's family gave a wry interpretation of his loss of vision. Absorbed in a book, they said, the boy walked into a moving streetcar: "Thomas Aquinas was to blame.")

✦ ✦ ✦

How could I write about religious figures who have served migrants and immigrants without mentioning Dorothy Day (1897–1980)? She motivated my grandparents to help start a Catholic Worker House of Hospitality in Cleveland. Later, my parents met and married under her watchful eye.

Servant of God Dorothy Day is being considered for canonization; her cause has been endorsed, unanimously, by the US bishops. Raised in a nonreligious family (her ancestry was European, and her family's religious background was Episcopalian), as an adult she experienced a spiritual conversion that led her to be baptized. Dorothy did not single out immigrants for her ministry per se, but she embraced them as belonging to the poor to whom she dedicated her service.

In recent years her letters and diaries have been published, as have excellent biographies. Here I simply focus on two images that I love.

The first picture that springs to my mind comes from her childhood. In her autobiography Dorothy wrote of exploring immigrant neighborhoods in Chicago. She had just read Upton Sinclair's *The Jungle,* about the meat-packing industry, which employed mainly foreign-born workers. Dorothy ventured into immigrant neighborhoods, pacing the streets with her baby brother in a stroller. Her eyes were opened to the cruelty of the city's poverty . . . but her senses were simultaneously engaged by the vitality she found there. "The odor of geranium leaves, tomato plants, marigolds; the smell of lumber, of tar, of roasting coffee; the smell of good bread and rolls and coffee cake coming from the small German bakeries. Here was enough beauty to satisfy me." Reading of the poor, of the workers, and walking the streets of Chicago she knew that "from that time on my life was to be linked to theirs, their interests were to be mine: I had received a call, a vocation, a direction to my life."[2]

The second image, also described in her autobiography, dates to a more complicated time in Dorothy's life. Baptized a Catholic, Dorothy separated from her common-law husband, the father of her only child. She continued to earn her living as a journalist while trying to put her newfound faith into practice.

In the winter of 1932, Dorothy traveled to Washington DC to cover a protest organized by the labor movement. It was December 8—the Feast of the Immaculate Conception—and she felt disturbed by the lack of Christian leadership. At the Hunger March she witnessed thousands of poor, working men and women walk for just wages, jobs, unemployment, and disability compensation. Many were immigrants and the children of immigrants. The church, Dorothy felt, must walk with them.

Entering the National Shrine of the Immaculate Conception, Dorothy offered an anguished prayer, asking God to guide her. Returning home, she met Peter Maurin, who began to instruct her in social doctrine. Together, they founded the Catholic Worker Movement.

Today, Catholic Worker Houses carry on their vision. Among their ministries (based on the works of mercy), many houses offer hospitality to refugees and immigrants—from Burma, Ghana, Mexico, El Salvador, Honduras, Guatemala, Iraq, Sudan, Afghanistan, and many more. Dorothy died in 1980, but her call, first heard in immigrant neighborhoods, continues to bear fruit.

✦ ✦ ✦

In the Southwest, Spanish-speaking Catholic communities predated the arrival of English-speaking missionaries, anchoring a constant Christian presence there for centuries. One contemporary

---

[2] Dorothy Day, *The Long Loneliness* (New York: Harper and Brothers, 1952), 37, 38. This book has never gone out of print, and it has been translated into numerous languages.

"saint" of the Southwest, a layman, lived a remarkable life of commitment to migrants.

Cesar Estrada Chavez was born in 1927 in Arizona, where his family lived in a small adobe house in farming country. When Chavez was a child, his grandparents lost their land during the Great Depression. Later, his father was taken advantage of in a shady business deal. The family was left with impossible interest debts and without the deed to their house. Finding themselves homeless, Chavez's family was forced to migrate in search of work.

Traveling through California, the Chavez family picked cotton in the fall, greens and peas in the winter, beans and cherries in the spring, and corn in the summer. They often slept in their car. Because they moved frequently, Chavez and his five siblings could not receive adequate schooling. Upon completing eighth grade, Chavez decided not to attend high school. He went to work in the fields so that his mother would not have to. After serving two years in the US Navy, Chavez returned to farm work and married. He and his wife, Helen, raised seven children.

Chavez discerned that social justice teaching dovetailed with the traditional Hispanic piety with which he had been raised. Priests and ministers influenced his faith, while community organizers introduced him to the principles of labor unionizing. He and other Mexican American leaders (notably, co-founder Dolores Huerta) began a labor association that came to be called the United Farm Workers. The union negotiated for improvements in working conditions and wages for their members, and it called attention to the plight of farm workers everywhere. Having himself lived the hardships that the union hoped to rectify, Chavez became a convincing spokesperson.

In his strategies Chavez followed closely the nonviolent philosophy of Mahatma Gandhi. He admired the work of contemporaries Martin Luther King Jr. and Dorothy Day (her last public act of civil disobedience took place at a farm-worker protest). He made his commitment to the cause visible through the practice of fasting.

Chavez's spirituality was also expressed through an unconventional practice. At that time, in his setting, vegetarianism was practically unheard of; Chavez would not eat meat. My carnivorous Italian American father visited Chavez in California. Upon learning that he was a vegetarian, my father asked why. Chavez pointed to a field of farm animals and responded lightly, "Do you see those animals? I like them better *that* way."

In the beginning Chavez opposed policies that favored immigration to the United States from Mexico; a ready supply of disenfranchised laborers would undermine the union's efforts to organize the workers who were already here. However, over time, Chavez and his colleagues began to advocate for undocumented immigrants' rights.

Leading a union required making hard decisions. Forming alliances with other organizations and settling disputes within the movement did not make for a smooth path, but it was one he tread steadfastly. Chavez died peacefully at the age of sixty-six in 1993, not far from the adobe home where his family once lived. He had been testifying in court that day on behalf of farm workers. He died during the night, lamp lit, a smile on his face, and a book on Native American crafts in his hand.

✢ ✢ ✢

Few readers would dispute that Mother Teresa of Calcutta is one of the most widely known religious figures of our time. Yet, if asked where she was from, most people would mistakenly respond, "India, of course—it says so in her name!" But contrary to popular belief, Mother Teresa was not a native of India. An immigrant became one of the most beloved faces of modern Christianity.

Born and raised in Albania, Agnes Gonxha Bojaxhiu entered the Sisters of Loreto, a missionary order, in Ireland, taking the religious name Teresa. Sent to India, Sister Teresa taught for many years. Her daily activities were confined to the sisters' convent and the boarding school they ran for girls.

During a railway trip to a retreat, Sister Teresa was stirred to the depths of her soul by the poverty and desperation she witnessed from her train window. After twenty years of religious life, Sister

Teresa exchanged her European-style Loreto habit for a white cotton, blue-lined sari. She picked up a dying beggar from the streets. She became *Mother* Teresa. And after spending almost two decades in India, she applied for citizenship.

Mother Teresa founded a new congregation, the Missionaries of Charity, because of this "call within a call."

I like to think that when Mother Teresa embraced her identity as an immigrant, God enlarged her heart. Taking on Indian dress and citizenship symbolized her immersion in her adopted homeland—but did not limit her identity or belonging. She would bear Christ's love to numerous countries. Entering into Indian reality opened her to a ministry that crossed borders. By the time of her death in 1997, Mother Teresa was loved by people all over the world.

In recent years Mother Teresa's inner struggles have been brought to light—making her an even more evocative figure. She wandered a spiritual desert yet resisted the temptation to renounce her steps. She clung to Christ, joining him on his Journey, the way of the cross. Recently I visited a convent of the Missionaries of Charity with a group of immigrants. We were deeply moved to read the words stenciled on the wall of their chapel: "I thirst."

✦ ✦ ✦

Religious leaders and faith-based organizations have served immigrants for centuries. Each time period and region develop unique narratives, but they tell of a common desire: to make a place, a spiritual home, for ourselves and others. Welcoming Christ in the stranger means undertaking a mutual journey toward one another. It also means setting down roots, together.

# Chapter Fifteen

# At Ellis Island

Who would have thought that I would learn as much as the students on a class trip? One balmy morning in late spring, my son's school visited Ellis Island.

In preparing for the trip the class researched the history of the island, which initially served as a military fortress for defense. They studied about Lady Liberty—herself an immigrant from France—whose pedestal was provided for through the efforts of Hungarian-born Joseph Pulitzer. They read the famous, emotive poem "The New Colossus" by Emma Lazarus, a descendant of Sephardic Jews from Portugal. They discussed the contributions of the millions of immigrant laborers who toiled in our country's industries, farms, and transportation. They marveled at the success of entrepreneurs such as Scottish-born Andrew Carnegie, whose drive and innovation led to new heights of prosperity. And . . . they were assigned to find out about any relatives who had come through Ellis Island.

The museum at Ellis Island documents the arrival of a total of twenty-two million immigrants, twelve million of whom came through this very port of entry. Over one hundred million Americans trace an ancestor to Ellis Island. My family and I are among them.

✦ ✦ ✦

It seemed fitting to visit Ellis Island with children, since in 1892, three young siblings were the first immigrants to enter the

United States here. Teenager Annie Moore and her two young brothers, seven and eleven years old, traveled from Ireland across the Atlantic to join their parents in New York. Their journey by steamship lasted ten days, during which Annie celebrated her fifteenth birthday.

On our trip the children loved the ferry and the views of Lady Liberty. They delighted in the choppy motions of the boat on the waves. They especially enjoyed the seagulls, which scooped up discarded snacks.

Arriving at the museum—renovated to resemble its appearance at the height of immigration—they were temporarily struck speechless by the impressive architecture of the main building. Even on a cloudy day, its large windows streamed with light. The expansive Registry Room (the Great Hall) imparted a sense of openness and possibility. I imagined my great-grandparents just arrived from Italy, lugging children and baggage up these steps through jostling crowds. An average of five thousand passengers traversed the Great Hall every day, reaching a peak of over eleven thousand people one April day in 1907.

The museum offers fascinating exhibits. One gallery shows black-and-white photos of newcomers' faces mounted along the walls. Another display contains items such as musical instruments, trunks and baggage, writing utensils, clothing, books and journals, shoes, and jewelry—belongings brought through Ellis Island and later donated to the museum by immigrants' families. At the Money Exchange, currency from different countries is pasted inside a glass wall for viewing. I jotted down the countries of origin of artifacts that caught my eye: Poland, Norway, Japan, Italy, Portugal, Germany, Hungary, Austria, Russia, Palestine, Crete, Ukraine, Jamaica, Trinidad, Switzerland, Romania, Lebanon, Turkey, and the French West Indies.

✢ ✢ ✢

My son and his classmates took for granted the rapidity with which newcomers were granted status. Having witnessed our contemporary immigration system, I was astonished. (Contrary to stereotype, the vast majority of today's migrants and immigrants are documented.)

First-class and second-class passengers were processed on board ship, but steerage travelers were taken by ferry or barge to the complex of buildings on Ellis Island. A team of doctors watched passengers climb the stairs, marking with chalk the clothing of anyone with obvious health problems. Arrivals diagnosed with ailments were housed in infirmaries for treatment. The property even held a maternity ward—where over 350 babies were born.

The legal component of the examination consisted of twenty-nine routine questions, such as name, hometown, destination, and the amount of money in a traveler's pocket. Answers were tersely—and sporadically—noted in the records. Only 1–2 percent were denied entry.

After a few hours, their medical and legal exams passed, the travelers descended the "stairs of separation," named so because a single set of steps led immigrants to different doors according to the final leg of their journey. About one-third of the arrivals remained in New York. Others moved on, mostly by train, to other destinations.

My grandmother's parents, Alessandra Cesare and Giovanni Caruso, had come from Italy's regions of Campagna and Molise, respectively, but as we prepared for the trip, I realized I knew very little else about them. We knew my grandmother was born here, in 1902 . . . but what year did my great-grandparents come through Ellis Island? For Alessandra, a widow, this was a second marriage. Had the older boys come separately in a previous passage with their father? When did her second husband arrive?

I thought that knowing my great-grandparents had embarked from Naples would make my search easier . . . but looking through the digitalized archives, I found that the majority of entries to Ellis Island had set out from Naples.

Life in Italy had always been hard for farmers, but toward the end of the century industry was encouraged and agriculture taxed disproportionately. Families like those of my father decided to emigrate. Opening photographs of records, I read in the category of "occupation" an overwhelming number of "peasants" or "farmers" (with sporadic mention of "servant" or "housewife," and an occasional "shoemaker" or "tailor").

My search for a record of my family brought up 651 Cesares, 7,147 Carusos, and 233 Giovanni Carusos. One possible candidate for my great-grandmother came in the listing of an illiterate woman who emigrated carrying six dollars in her pocket (a fellow traveler carried even less than two dollars). However, the dates did not match up; this Cesare arrived later than the year of my grandmother's birth. Another entry that might have been that of my great-grandmother described a woman traveling with a daughter. On closer inspection the records listed the daughter as much older than my grandmother's sister would have been.

Many records, if not most, contained incomplete handwritten information garnered through interpreters. Over thirty languages were translated at Ellis Island. Details were routinely omitted for the sake of faster processing. Last names were notoriously misspelled or even changed. While my family is absolutely certain that our ancestors came through Ellis Island, I could not definitively identify their records.

I do know that my grandmother's family settled in an Italian neighborhood in walking proximity to the island. They quickly adapted to their new life in New York. My grandmother—the second youngest child of her parents' large family—never set foot in Italy. Her sisters worked for the garment industry. Her brothers entered the workforce at twelve or fourteen years of age as masons and bricklayers. Family lore boasts that one of them, who was enormously strong, single-handedly set the Prometheus statue in place at Rockefeller Center.

The working members of the family brought home their pay to my great-grandmother, the matriarch of the clan. Attempting to preserve customs from the old country, she objected not only to the idea of her children marrying non-Italians, but even non-*mainland* Italians. It took a major battle to convince her to accept a daughter's marriage to a Sicilian.

My spirited grandmother felt stifled in her parents' home and neighborhood. In a bid for freedom, she eloped; however, the marriage did not last. Thankfully, by the time my grandmother met my grandfather, her mother had set aside some of her rigidity. After all, her other daughter's marriage to a Sicilian had worked out well. My great-grandmother was charmed by the handsome American who won over my grandmother. A smooth conversationalist and a dapper dresser, my grandfather loved to travel. On their first date, just returned from Florida, he carried a baby alligator in his suit-coat pocket.

Although at first they had resisted outsiders' marrying into the clan, my grandmother's family was fascinated by my grandfather's confident manner. He moved about freely in the country to which they did not yet fully belong. Partly English, with a British surname, he explained that his mother's family was Irish. (Over the course of her life, my grandmother married three Irishmen. She later joked, "I don't know if I couldn't get enough of a good thing, or if it was a bad habit I just couldn't break.")

My grandfather made no secret of the challenges of introducing his Italian wife to the social circles he frequented. He enjoyed the family gatherings back in the old neighborhood—complete with several courses of food, plenty of good wine, and fancy liqueurs—but had no intention of living there. His ancestors, Thomas and Rebecca Cornell, came from England in 1637. They lived next door to Anne Hutchinson in Rhode Island. His mother's people came much later, when the Irish were swept by the Great Hunger across the ocean to the United States, and Ann McDonald's family settled in the Northeast.

My father says of his mother, "Her project was to become an American." She shortened the glorious Antonietta to plain Ann. Speaking English without an accent, she claimed not to know Italian . . . although two glasses of wine would make her Neapolitan fluent. She studied for one year of high school and one year of secretarial school, after which she worked briefly for an Italian import company.

Like my mother's forebears a century earlier, my father's family proved their loyalty to the United States by joining the Armed

Forces. My father's uncles served in the Army during the First World War, and three cousins in the Second. After the Service, they got jobs in real estate, in the postal service, in pharmacies, and in businesses serving Italian American communities. Some chose to remain within these circles. Others moved into the wider society. With the Second World War, by and large, anti-Italian prejudice melted.

✦ ✦ ✦

Two centuries ago Benjamin Franklin worried that an influx of German immigrants would overrun the United States. Their language and customs were so foreign, he fretted. One hundred years later, the wave of "new" immigrants of the time—Poles, Italians, Russians, and Jews of various countries—were thought too different to ever assimilate. Exhibits at Ellis Island remind visitors of an unfortunate trend. With the exception of Native Americans, people in the United States are descended from immigrants, and yet each firstborn generation seems to erase the memory of its parents' arrival.

History shows that the tendency to accept or exclude immigrants went hand in hand with the demand for labor. For example, Chinese immigrants were employed to build railroads, but once these were built, the Chinese Exclusion Act of 1882 restricted their entry into the United States.

And at the turn of the century, especially in cities, industrialization demanded labor.

At the museum, a plaque commemorates the 146 women who died in the Shirtwaist Fire in 1911. The Triangle Waist Company hired young immigrants like my grandmother's sisters, mostly from Italy and Eastern Europe, to sew fashionable ladies' blouses. When a fire broke out in the New York City factory, workers were trapped behind locked doors (a routine practice, supposedly to prevent theft). Terrified workers died from burns, asphyxiation, or injuries from jumping out windows. Two of them were only fourteen years old.

Once the need for labor diminished, the US population was perceived as saturated. Already weak sympathy toward immigrants waned even more. Ellis Island reflected changing trends.

In 1921, the First Quota Act sharply reduced admissions from Southern and Eastern European countries, slowing the traffic of immigrants through the island. Starting in 1925, petitions had to be introduced for processing in immigrants' countries of origin. With the Great Depression, the number of immigration petitions plummeted. There was no work with the economy in shambles.

During World War II, Japanese, Italian, and German families were interned at Ellis Island. The Great Hall served as a recreational area. Later, even this use was discontinued. The island was closed in 1954.

Exhibits document not only the opening but also the closing of Ellis Island. Photos from that time show a property in ruin. The buildings and the land fell into serious decline. Neglect of Ellis Island seemed to represent the public desire to forget about immigration in general. Only in the 1980s did interest arise in the restoration of this historic site. It was opened to the public in 1990 after a valiant campaign of renovation.

My husband and I have been involved in advocacy for migrants and immigrants for twenty years. In one project we are blessed to serve with an Irish American brother whose parents emigrated from "home" to the Bronx. When giving a presentation, he invariably begins: "In the people we serve, I see the faces of my own father and mother."

Visiting Ellis Island, I see the faces of my ancestors in the photos hung on its gallery walls. My forebears had much in common with today's displaced emigrants. They responded to the "pull" of garment factories and construction, railroads and canals in the same way today's immigrants come, seeking work. These past decades have also seen millions of arrivals. From Mexico, the Latin American country I know best, emigration reached heights comparable to those of the times of my European ancestors.

But the phenomenon is already slowing—due to Mexico's declining birth rate and lower availability of US jobs. As our economy falters, fewer arrive. As development improves abroad, other countries' citizens emigrate less. Immigration waves are precisely that—waves.

Contemporary debates on immigration would sound familiar to my great-grandparents. Like each incoming population, they followed strategies of resistance or assimilation particular to their cultural backgrounds and their times. Unwittingly, they passed on contradictory messages to their descendants about our ethnic identities. I lament the loss of languages: Italian, Slovenian, Irish. Mostly I regard with awe their enormous efforts to organize trade unions, parishes, small businesses, and civic associations. Marred by migrant mourning and disinheritance, nevertheless their lives were guided by faith. Landing at Ellis Island, they brought their determination to make the most of this nation's tremendous possibilities.

✦ ✦ ✦

Leaving Ellis Island, my son's class was exhausted. The children slept most of the bus ride home. I stayed awake, mind and heart full.

# Chapter Sixteen

# Pure Grace

I end this book with two stories. One took place over fifty years ago; the other, last week.

The first was told to me by a friend who specializes in family and immigration policy. When she was a child, her own parents emigrated as World War II refugees from Latvia. She recounts the following experience:

> "My parents settled in a camp in northern France. For nine years they lived in an old army barrack with no indoor plumbing and a coal stove for heat. When my mother became pregnant with me there was no hope of going to a French hospital—compassion fatigue had set in and no one wanted these 'displaced persons' around. Medical care was administered in the camp; there wasn't much of it. The camp doctor did not show up until three days after I was born. I was premature and very small. He took one look at me, said, 'Don't bother naming it,' and left."

Granted refugee-resettlement visas, the family left the camp to make their home the United States. As a young woman this friend began to work with immigrants, pursuing a career in social work. She raised a family and advanced in her professional life. She learned the story of her birth decades later:

> "I did not know this story until I was in my mid-fifties. I was moving my mother's stuff and one box held old photographs

of us in the French refugee camp. I never knew these photographs existed. I asked my mother why she never showed them to me or talked much about that time. She responded, 'What was there to tell?' Which says it all."

She further reflected, "No person should be referred to as 'it'—if you come into this world you have a name, and my lifelong work has been to give voice to that."

✤ ✤ ✤

The second story took place quite recently. I received a call one Sunday morning from friends in a town further upstate, where Spanish-speaking services are not readily available. A woman was about to be discharged from the hospital. She and her husband, newcomers who are both from El Salvador, had been expecting a child. Their pregnancy ended suddenly and unexpectedly with the premature delivery of a stillborn.

The staff wanted the bed for incoming patients. It was time to say goodbye to the stillborn, who would be left at the hospital.

Any family would feel bereavement . . . this couple bore the added burden of migratory mourning. They had come to this country to provide a better life for their children, yet they had lost a child. The unfamiliar hospital setting felt forbidding because of language and cultural differences. Relatives circled the young parents with support, yet they too felt acutely aware of being far from home.

Before leaving, the family needed to know that their grief—and the life of their little one—*mattered.*

A question weighed on their minds. As a stillborn, the baby would not be baptized. They would arrange a memorial mass later, but this might take several days. The family wanted to know, when would their child receive a name?

I walked into the hospital room to find a quiet bundle wrapped in a blanket surrounded by grieving family members. During our simple prayer I marked her little, cold forehead with the Sign of the Cross. I could not baptize her, but I reminded her relatives of

Jesus' words, "Let the little children come to me" (Mt 19:14; cf. Mk 10:13–16; Lk 18:15–17). I sprinkled her parents with holy water, asking for their healing. The first time I pronounced the name they had chosen for their daughter, an audible shudder of relief swept through the room. As we continued, the family members breathed more and more deeply with each mention of her name.

✦ ✦ ✦

A host of witnesses—individuals and organizations, families and institutions, neighbors and professionals—rejoice in migrants' and immigrants' names. New Americans give voice to where they come from, what they bring with them . . . and their hopes for themselves and their children. I do my best to listen. They will make their way, as our ancestors did, but they will do so in their own ways . . . and perhaps in new ones. This opens a horizon of possibilities. I offer my *granito de arena* (grain of sand) alongside those of other men and women of faith who insist that migrants and immigrants *matter.*

Looking back after twenty years on a ministry that has been both incredibly challenging and immensely rewarding, I return to moments like this one—moments of pure grace. Entering that hospital room, I was overtaken by a familiar rush: the cresting of a wave of gratitude. Once again, my heart overflows.

✦ ✦ ✦

At the time of this writing, our federal and state governments wrestle with the practical and legal implications of immigration. Congress debates how to secure our borders—an issue of paramount importance. The rising tide of violence along the US-Mexico border poses grave concern, as does the threat of terrorism. (It is worth noting, however, that none of the perpetrators of the 9/11 attacks entered the United States illegally.)

The United States is only one nation among many that grapple with these issues. Many developed countries face intensified immigration. We easily think of Los Angeles, New York, and Miami as cities with high proportions of foreign-born inhabitants, but what about Dubai and Mecca, Toronto and Vancouver? Amsterdam, The Hague, Auckland? At Lempadusa, since Pope Francis' papal visit, at least 350 migrants have drowned.

Colleagues in ministry and social services tell their own stories. The International Grail Movement enabled me to join in these discussions. A Dutch acquaintance works to rescue women enslaved by human trafficking. She knows firsthand how difficult it is to break the cycle of violence when victims live in fear of civil authorities.

An Australian spoke to me of the deaths of twenty-seven asylum seekers whose vessel crashed on the rocks off of Christmas Island. Tragically, these men, women, and children fleeing poor, war-torn countries would be neither the first nor the last to die on the same rocks. When she asked rhetorically, "When will this end? What can be done?" she voiced the thoughts of concerned people in many parts of the world.

Congress also currently debates how to normalize the status of millions of undocumented people already living and working in the United States. Advocates posit the advantages of making them permanent residents, at the very least. A "path to citizenship" would open further channels leading to naturalization for those who qualify.

On a state level some local governments have enacted legislation to make life extremely difficult for undocumented immigrants. Ironically, efforts to make communities "secure" or "safe" often have detrimental effects. Families are torn apart, with relatives ruthlessly detained and deported. Heightened tension between law enforcement and immigrant neighborhoods makes residents less likely to report crime. Schools empty of students. High-tech business, among others, suffer because of the lack of skilled labor. Small-business owners lose employees for the low-paying jobs that only migrants and immigrants will fill.

Several states have taken bold steps in the opposite direction. For example, provisions in several states now allow all drivers of motor vehicles—regardless of immigration status—to become authorized license holders. On a national level a whole generation of young people is becoming empowered to work and study. A first step has been taken through Deferred Action for Childhood Arrivals. Someday soon, these young adults will be fully integrated through legislation such as The Dream Act. Brought here in their childhood, the "dreamers" who were once undocumented will advocate for their parents.

A "dreamer" I have known since her childhood wrote in a letter to me from California:

> I was brought to the United States when I was three years old. Coming from a migrant family, I have no real stability, no way of planning for my future. I lack what many take for granted. How can I contribute to the economy and social progress without getting educated? I want to give back to my community. How can I assume leadership without risking everything I have worked for? Can I obtain respect for myself and not be discriminated against when I am forced to stay in the shadows? This legislation would allow me to truly *live* my dream and make it a *reality*. I am one of many young adults searching for a way to excel. Not only am I looking to survive, I am also looking to thrive.

As another friend who works with migrants and immigrants likes to say, "The golden door of Emma Lazarus's poem may open and close . . . but it is not locked." Each year new Americans from every nation on the globe are sworn in. In communities across this continent heroic efforts for the integration of immigrants are undertaken every day.

Setting down roots—establishing belonging and deepening our sense of place—remains a fundamental priority for individuals and peoples. But mobility has been part of our history since human beings stood upright.

The most fundamental plot of sacred scripture, salvation history, unfolds through stories of migration. With all its hardships, human mobility serves as a paradigm of religious faith. Christians espouse belief in a Savior who embodied migration in his lifetime—and who continues to cross borders as the risen Lord. In migration, we find a source of blessing.

Thirty-three Hispanic American bishops of the United States released an open letter to undocumented immigrants on December 12, 2011 (the Feast of Our Lady of Guadalupe). In it, they thanked immigrants for the many gifts they bring to the United States and to the church. They wrote, "You reveal to us the supreme reality of life: we are all migrants."

Our faith can be renewed when we meditate on Jesus' life and mission in relation to migration. We awaken to the fundamental truth of God's great love, crossing barriers with awesome power. We recognize how in his person, Jesus took on the migrant identity of his people. We feel compelled to imitate his adventurous ministry—because that is where we will find him. We meet Jesus Christ again in salvation history. The scriptures come alive with fresh insight.

Once we acknowledge migration in the Bible as both a sociological reality and as a mother lode of spiritual metaphors, we enrich our own encounters with these sacred texts. As we wonder at their revelatory significance for their original audiences of the past, we open ourselves to God's *living* word: the revelatory meaning they hold for us in our own contexts. Following the Jewish biblical tradition, Christian communities search scriptures and tradition in order to discern authentic clues as to where the gospel might be leading them.[1]

Human mobility is a "sign of the times," a phenomenon that reveals our world today. As globalization accelerates the pace of emigration, people of various faiths draw from their respective traditions. These convictions can sustain us as we work in various ways toward the reconciliation. How *could* it be easy to forge laws and attitudes that take such complexity into account?

---

[1] For Catholic teaching, see Donald Kerwin and Jill Marie Gerschutz, eds., *And You Welcomed Me: Catholic Social Teaching and Migration* (Lanham, MD: Lexington Books, 2009).

Our hearts can become pure, even if our policies cannot. Our borders cannot be open . . . but our hearts can. Our country continues to receive new citizens. Our cities, towns, and neighborhoods welcome new neighbors. Our churches and other faith communities serve as spiritual homes. We, too, can migrate. We can move closer to the gospel vision of justice and peace.

And . . . we can take steps, steps toward Christ in the stranger. Mine have been mapped out by the works of mercy. And by these words, words that led me to the side of a hospital bed in a maternity ward:

> Then the king will say to those at his right hand, "Come, you that are blessed by my Father, inherit the kingdom prepared for you from the foundation of the world; for I was hungry and you gave me food, I was thirsty and you gave me something to drink, I was a stranger and you welcomed me, I was naked and you gave me clothing, I was sick and you took care of me, I was in prison and you visited me." (Mt 25:34–36)